Mossback

Mossback

Ecology, Emancipation, and
Foraging for Hope in Painful Places

DAVID MICHAEL PRITCHETT

Foreword by J. Drew Lanham

Trinity University Press
San Antonio, Texas

Trinity University Press
San Antonio, Texas 78212

Cover design by Derek Thornton / Notch Design
Book design by Amnet
Cover art: Stocksy, 2341641; Shutterstock, 298514801, 2031867635
Author photo by Ben Travers

ISBN 978-1-59534-991-0 paper
ISBN 978-1-59534-992-7 ebook

Trinity University Press strives to produce its books using methods and materials
in an environmentally sensitive manner. We favor working with manufacturers
that practice sustainable management of all natural resources, produce paper using
recycled stock, and manage forests with the best possible practices for people,
biodiversity, and sustainability. The press is a member of the Green Press Initiative, a
nonprofit program dedicated to supporting publishers in their efforts to reduce their
impacts on endangered forests, climate change, and forest-dependent communities.

The paper used in this publication meets the minimum requirements of the
American National Standard for Information Sciences—Permanence of Paper for
Printed Library Materials, ansi 39.48–1992.

CIP data on file at the Library of Congress

27 26 25 24 23 | 5 4 3 2 1

For Ty and Cole,
Chloé and Max,
Stig and Soren

May you find yourselves always among kin

CONTENTS

FOREWORD

J. Drew Lanham

What does wilderness hide? What does it reveal? Most of what we know of wildness in America has come through a homogenized filter of white privileged men. Men bent first on subduing the untamed vastness of the continent, driving by genocide and policy the indigenous who, without western science or manifest destiny, knew the land and lived by it. This is not to say there was some perfect before the intrusion of colonialism, but there were people that whiteness would not tolerate. Fast forward not too far from ideas of forest primeval, and White America demanded free labor to till the land and maximize profit. Enter about 1619, enslavement. Africans brought to this land as unwilling immigrants to do the bidding of conquerors. And so we did. We girdled the mammoth oaks, cypress, tupelo, gum, and sycamore to lay waste to forest that would become fields. Black Africans skilled at engineering tidal control ditched, trunked, and gated brackish water to rise and fall within inches of desired levels as the great sylvan swaths of bottomland hardwood forest on the southeastern Atlantic coastal plain gave way to rice cultivation.

In the deeper South, cane fields grew. Whiteness prospered and Blackness suffered. And on the margins where wildness remained, things remained hidden. Here, where moss hung from the same trees where Black necks were sometimes stretched, and where moss-covered logs might hide a viper, Black folks found sustenance from hunting and gathering. With often meager rations provided, swamps were whole food markets. Too, Black folks found solace there. We prayed in woodland temples. And some of us stayed there. The woods became homeplaces, refuges. Safe spaces to move between watchful eyes and wanted posters offering rewards for "lurking negroes." The wild was not a recreation choice but a requisite for survival in chattel society.

Hiding to reveal true self. The ancestors often found bits and pieces of freedom in foreboding places. And many claimed their freedom by personal emancipation proclamation. Abolitionist activist Harriet Tubman is among those best known for finding freedom in wildness. The woods may not have been so lovely, but they were appropriately dark and deep, providing cover for escape. It took a certain set of skills to survive in swamps and forest and field. Long before wilderness was made the exclusive destination of the privileged decked out in expensive technical gear, Harriet found her way through and blazed trails for others with intelligence and wit packed in burlap sacks.

Harriet watched the stars

by brain and faith made the astronomically correct calculus that
would analyze the algorithms of liberty regressed against
bondage and chains.

Her only solution was escape.

No, not escape—

SELF-LIBERATION!

The equation was to know the way by nature.

Moss on the free side.

Follow the Drinking Gourd's handle to the river crossing.

When the rising sun is on the right shoulder

that way be east.

Listen for the marsh hens calling in the sweetgrass.

Take that way to the boats on the Combahee.

Else walk against the water flow.

Stay far as you can from where the cat owl calls

on the high ground—

that's where the bloodhounds easy smell

your runnin' fear

to catch freedom's scent.

Walk quiet as dewfall on cotton.

Run fast by dark on the trail

the buck deer lay down.

Make the dogs think you is his rut stank.

Take that pissed-up mud where he dug

'neath the lickin' branch.

Rub it all over.

Now be whitetail and carry on.

Stay deep down in the swamp until the first light.

When the longbeard turkey gobble on the roost mean mornin'
   comin' soon
hide inside the ol' hollow cypress then.
The green and yellow birds they call parakeets
know you ain't there to hurt 'em.
Lay still. Be quiet.
The parrot gon' leave first light.
It will be dark when time to travel again.
Eat the seeds the parrots drop.
It's a gift they give.
Track to the low wet place
where the cottonmouth lie thick and mean
where the white men are scared to go.
Be quiet until the monkey owl hoot that evenin'—
"HOOOAWWWWWW! HOOOHOOOAWWWWWW!"
That be me.
Harriet calling you to come on.
Find the gourd in the inkin' blue sky
—then do it all again.
Till you cross the river to the free side.

And so Harriet moss-backed herself and untold numbers
of others through a wilderness that was both foe and friend.
She knew how to hide in plain sight. How to read the woods.
How to play the light. Herein, the moss-backed denizens of
southeastern wilderness are shown to us in a truer light than
many have ever known.

   It should cause the reader to rethink Black association (or
dissociation) with "the outdoors" and wildness as American
conservation and environmentalism currently define them.

We are "out there" for the same reasons but also different ones than those of our white brothers, sisters, and others. We often aren't "out there" because of a deep cultural trauma that has not been adequately addressed or assuaged by the "just get outdoors" crowd. There is clear dissonance and obvious intimacy in this history.

Mossback is a fat lighter knot, lit to torch burning bright in the intellectual night. Here's to a deeper and more nuanced expedition, a more enlightened view, into what being Black and wild portends.

MOSSBACK

I step out of the car. It is only mid-May, not the high temperature of summer, but already the air hangs thickly with a wet heat. The air has a smell of sweet rot. A turmeric light filters through cedar, cypress, maple, and pine, and the ground is dark with moist soil. Green carpets of moss crawl up the leggy trunks of trees standing in turbid patches of water. The place is aptly named: this is Dismal Swamp, on the eastern border of Virginia and North Carolina. I drove from the North Carolina coast to get here, hugging the edge of the swamp as I followed roads tracing the border around to the western edge where there is vehicle access to Lake Drummond in the middle of the protected area.

In his book *The Art of Not Being Governed*, James C. Scott describes the concept of "rough terrain." Throughout history, certain geographies and ecologies served as places of escape from empires, because they were places that empires could not efficiently control. Dismal Swamp, here at the border of North Carolina and Virginia, is a rough terrain of sorts, where fugitive enslaved people could escape. So, too, were the vast snowy regions of northern Europe and Asia, where indigenous people could remain protected by harsh winters, relatively unaffected by civilizations to their south. Scott's study focuses on Southeast Asia, in a vast mountainous area that offered a rough terrain to harbor people fleeing lowland empires. There the steep mountainsides could not be farmed for grains, and the roads could not be built for large-scale transport of goods. I've come to this swamp because I am fascinated by rough terrain, by learning from ways people have escaped. I want to learn from maroons and other absconded folks how to get away.

I look around, but immediately I am swarmed with an array of insects. To my right I see a boardwalk floating above the muddy ground. I head toward it, and soon my footsteps are thudding across the raised path. I swat at the buzzing around my head as I walk to the information booth. Along the boardwalk, I watch spiders creep between the planks and underneath. A grackle calls unseen in the muggy woods, its sound like the high screech of a microphone feedback. The landscape varies. It is all flat, but some areas have standing water, while others are simply damp mud. In other spots I intuit from the dried and bleached-out algae lying across the ground that there was once standing water here. I stop to take a picture, then look down, only to realize that mosquitos have blanketed my legs with their winged hunger for blood. I swat them away and resolve to keep in motion to minimize the feedings.

One hundred and twelve thousand acres of wetland are currently preserved under the Dismal Swamp Act of 1974, but the original swamp is estimated to have been ten times the present size. The swamp featured as a place full of wealth and symbolic power within the imaginations of the white settlers' minds. From early in colonial history the swamp was seen as a resource—George Washington formed a partnership of investors in 1763 who hoped to drain the swamp, harvest the trees for lumber, and then use the land for farming. The group managed to create a five-mile ditch from the western edge of the swamp to Lake Drummond, a massive endeavor done with enslaved labor. This did not accomplish the goal of draining the swamp, but it did create a path inward that companies could use to transport timber.

Though the swamp was a large natural resource, it also was seen as a threat to the settlers' society. It was long known as a refuge for maroons escaping slavery. After Nat Turner's rebellion in 1831, many of the white communities assumed he had gone to Dismal Swamp, and they feared he would incite the maroon communities to emerge from the swamp to continue a campaign across the South. Although he did not hide there, this fear speaks to the swamp's symbolic power: A place that could not be tamed. A dark ecosystem that harbored escaped slaves.

Historians believe that the swamp at times harbored more than two thousand maroons. They established small colonies, sometimes up to forty acres in size, on raised ground within the swamp's borders. According to Daniel Sayers, an anthropologist who has long studied the maroons of Dismal Swamp, these villages had their own economies and cultural systems.[1] Maroon communities thrived for more than two centuries in this brackish but vibrant place. Despite a few canals penetrating into parts of the swamp, it was still so thick with mud and growth that in the heart of slavery, entire generations lived there without seeing a white person. For formerly enslaved people, this was a liberating ecology.

Abolitionist James Redpath recorded an interview in Canada with a refugee slave named Charlie who spent time in Dismal Swamp.[2] For Charlie, even though the swamp was "all dreary like," where "dar never was any heaven's sunshine in parts," the marsh was a haven. He describes how, united by common interest and fugitive status, swamp residents looked out for one another and worked together: "All 'gree as if dey had only one head and one heart, with hunder legs and hunder hands." The place had been a site of refuge for so long that Charlie met adults who had grown up in the swamp and never seen a white person. Of the water, Charlie reports that it was the best "ever tasted by man."

What was the sweet water of freedom for maroons was bitter tincture to others. William Byrd II of Virginia, tasked with surveying the dividing line between Virginia and North Carolina, complained of the swamp water, "It was far from being clear or well-tasted, and besides had a Physical Effect, from the Tincture it receiv'd from the effects of the Roots and Shrubbs and Trees that grew in the Neighborhood."[3] He further lamented, "Never was Rum, that cordial of Life, more necessary than it was in this Dirty Place."[4]

But Dismal Swamp, maroon refuge, was only one of many dank swamps of the Carolinas. Poor white folks also lived in many of these wetland areas, scratching out a living by trap and scrap. These folks came to be called mossbacks, a pejorative term suggesting that they moved so slowly among the cypress that moss grew on their clothing. This sense of the term is also used to describe large fish and turtles, similarly so slow moving that a layer of algae (which looks like moss) grows on their backs.

During the Civil War, many Confederate draft dodgers and deserters hid out in the swamps and other marginal areas to escape military service. The word also came to be used to describe these men, who, often of similar socioeconomic background to the original mossbacks, lived in backwoods and swamps during the war. Historian William Oates records an instance of this use of the term: "Robert Medlock was 23 years old when he enlisted August 15, 1862. Served well for a time and then deserted, went home, and became a moss-back."[5]

These men were against the war for many reasons, but often because they saw that it was largely a war led by plantation-owning elites who did not want the economic losses associated with abolition of slavery. This stance was seen as reactionary and stubborn, and thus *mossback* came to connote what it does today: a conservative or reactionary person who is so set in their ways, so sedentary of thought, that moss grows on their backs.

Mossback also seems to have taken on a broader political meaning, at least for a while, of those against southern white elites. This is hinted at in an 1872 report to Congress. In response to concerns about the Ku Klux Klan organizing in the former Confederate States, a committee was formed to look into the problem. One case reported was from Fayette County in Alabama, wherein Second Lieutenant John Bateman describes "a party of men known as the Ku Klux have been committing depredations." He relates that "to counteract this an Anti-Ku-Klux party has been organized, styling themselves 'Mossy-backs.'"[6] The conflict between the two organizations led to a shootout, wounding at least two men and killing a third.

Indigenous ecologist Robin Wall Kimmerer, who studies mosses, writes, "There is an ancient conversation going on between mosses and rocks, poetry to be sure. About light and shadow and the drift of continents."[7] There is also something sensual about moss. Have you ever stepped with bare feet on a cool bed of moss under the columns of tall trees? It feels like a living carpet, like a thousand tiny grasses bending to the weight of your body and caressing your skin. It is what philosopher and biologist Andreas Weber might call an experience of erotic ecology.[8]

I want to reclaim this term *mossback*. It paints an image of a person united with their environment, a person moving slowly enough to listen—a person with that selfsame poetry of rock and moss being written in live green script across their backs. A mossback would naturally be conservative—that is, would seek to protect the land and relations it depends on. A mossback would understand interdependence by virtue of their union with bryophytes. Someone comfortable with moss on their back might also be comfortable with an existence separate from the frenzied pace of the plantation economy. In fact, they might even resist a society willing to enslave other humans or to send young humans to war for profit. While a maroon is an escaped slave, a mossback might be the analogous term of someone who has relatively more social power. A mossback is not an enslaved person who escaped but a person who actively rejects participation in an enslaving society.

After a few stops and walks in the swamp, I drive all the way to Lake Drummond. A short pier takes me partway over the lake. The water is shallow, with cypress standing around the edge of the swamp. They say that the tannins from so many cedar and cypress keep the water brown-hued but clean and pure. The lake water was considered medicinal due to the tannins' antibacterial properties. I kneel down on the pier and immerse my hand in the water; it is cool and refreshing. I'm tempted to take a drink, but I'm too averse to the risk of waterborne illness, despite the tannins. Instead I offer a short prayer:

> Water of refuge, water of life.
> Teach me to value dismal things, to find in darkness freedom.
> Help me to listen to dark ecologies,
> let the poetry of places I inhabit grow on me
> as I grow within it.
> Let my back be mossy
> my habits full of care and attention,
> and my politics guided by liberation.

Soon I walk back to my car and drive the Washington ditch from the heart of the swamp back to the western edge. I only had an afternoon in the swamp, time only for a brief glimpse, a fleeting aesthetic of the place. During the drive back to the coast where I am staying, I have time to reflect on the deep history and symbolism of the place. I think of this place as a refuge from those on the run from a plantation economy based on slavery.

My mind ferments and questions bubble up: Are there still liberating ecologies today, rough terrains not yet completely controlled by the economy that has devastated so much of the globe? I think about how many enslaved people died to build the ditch and berm that allowed me to access the swamp.

What are we willing to sacrifice for resources? What are the stories about the world we are willing to inhabit? Is the earth a resource or a relationship? Who do we consider inferior, and who do we consider kin? I scratch at bites from mosquitos and wonder what I would be willing to endure in order to escape. I think about the water as a litmus. I wasn't thirsty enough to risk a drink but have certainly been in situations where I was willing to drink any water, no matter the amount of particulates, to slake my thirst. How thirsty must we be for freedom? How does desire for life animate our choices? Is it better to rebel, or abscond, when faced with unacceptable conditions? And how often do we get to make such a choice? These are the questions I explore in the book you hold in your hands. Answering them requires seeing ourselves and the places we inhabit in new ways.

The landscapes we call home continually change. Slow and relatively stable forces, like geologic events and weather, shape a place, but so too does the culture that emerges from the many creatures living and interacting with the terrain. A landscape has a geologic history of minuscule tectonic shifts or sudden explosive volcanic activity, has a natural ecological history of plant and animal communities shifting over time, and has a human history of living with and interacting with a place. This long process has left us with the places we love. A mile-deep canyon. Meadows edged with forest, thick with berries. The long spine of the Sierras. Prairie expanse. The curve at your favorite swimming spot in the creek.

But human activity in the last two centuries has dramatically increased the rate of change. Humans have surpassed geological forces in shaping the earth. Through deforestation, increasing atmospheric carbon, and creating urban heat islands, humans have changed weather patterns. In North America, colonization by Europeans altered the landscape. Forests were clear-cut for timber and for agriculture. Mines continue to leave lacerating scars. Overhunting of beavers changed the structures of rivers and wetlands. Cultural burning practices, in which indigenous people kept forests healthy and meadows vibrant through regular low-intensity burns, were prohibited or simply stopped when indigenous people were displaced, leaving the woods overgrown and tangled. Lakes have been drained, rivers dammed, and water tables emptied.

If it is useful to learn how history and political structures have shaped the places we inhabit, it also makes sense to think about how history has shaped our understanding of our own selves. The body is itself a landscape. We have our own bony ridges, soft hills, and meandering valleys. We bear scars from our weathered histories. Psychological wounds, too, impact how we think, how we act. The external forces of our lives—the kind of food we have access to, the environment we inhabit—shape the biota that inhabit our skin, our guts. Likewise, cultural patterns affect our identity by making stories about our bodies. Social and political factors tell us which bodies are beautiful, what other bodies our own flesh can love.

My own body is overlaid with a story inherited from a particular historical narrative. I descend from European ancestors who came to the Americas for a variety of reasons. Across the centuries they came to understand themselves as white. That whiteness was cast in contrast to others, who were seen as black- or brown-skinned. In the United States, to become racialized white meant one had to reject much of the uniqueness of the German, Irish, English, or other European culture one came from. The word *deracinate* means "to pull up from the root." Etymology does not seem to tie this word to the similar word *race*, but it is easy to read whiteness as a deracination. The privileges associated with whiteness came at the cost of one's sense of belonging. To become white was to lose one's roots.

Our landscapes, our bodies, and our psyches need healing. Modern medicine, the healing modality I am trained in, operates by the axiom that diagnosis precedes prescription. It's difficult to treat the infection unless you know what pathogen caused it. *Diagnosis* means "recognizing a disease from its symptoms" and comes from Greek roots *dia* + *gnosis*, meaning "to know thoroughly." The better we see and understand the current pathologies of our world, I wager, the more likely we can work to heal them. This book employs a variety of lenses to help see problems and causes more clearly. I will not give prescriptions, but I hope to offer insights into our situation and point toward possibilities for healing.

The search for symptoms and etiologies of our pathologies spans much of the globe. As a child, I lived in the shadow of Mount Kenya, and mountains continue to loom in my psyche. I write about encounters on Mount Kilimanjaro, the foothills of Mount Kenya, Mount Hood in Oregon, and the Ozarks of Arkansas. Water, too, features prominently throughout the book, from desert wetland oases to swamps, to the river of my own watershed. Desert landscapes offer places of learning about myself, and the agricultural plains of the Midwest—not arid but still deserts of monocropping—teach me about the way colonialism has shaped the broader landscape. The word *learn* is etymologically related to the word *lore*, and both are based on the proto-Germanic word *leornian*, meaning "to get knowledge." The even earlier root word, linguists suggest, is the Indo-European *leis*, which means "to track." A trail, as many have pointed out, is its own chronicle, a tale told by hoof and paw in the textured grains of the landscape. Story itself, some have theorized, has its origin in the bardic retelling of the hunt around a fire. And herein lie the roots of my own learning: by following the story lines of folklore, we learn the ancient wisdom, passed down through narrative arc and poetic tongue, of how to live well in situ. By following trails, we learn about the living, nonhuman kin who inhabit the same world and through whom we might better understand how to live well ourselves in these same storied places.

Stories shape us. From the origin of the universe to the founding of a nation, cosmologies tell us how to understand the world, its order, and our own place within it. In Ancient Mesopotamia, the world was created by the violent slaying of Tiamat. Rome was famously founded by Romulus after he killed his brother. The settling of the American West was buttressed by the "story" of Manifest Destiny, which said that it was the divine right of the United States to colonize North America from East to West Coasts. So many of our cosmologies begin with violence. To see the world differently, we need different stories. Sometimes this means reading traditional stories in a new light, as I do with some Judeo-Christian stories. In other places, this means looking for new tales that help us see the world we inhabit in different ways. Folklore and myth help to expand our world by bringing in other voices. In search of better cosmologies, I go to these mythic places:

stories where fish become women, witches eat children, poets become stags, humans make deals with devils. If mossbacks reject the cosmologies that allow for enslaving humans, or for sending young men to die in wars, they must also find new stories or reclaim old ones. They need different cosmologies than the ones that lead to plantation economies to shape how they understand the world.

There are no easy answers, but my encounters in this book with myth, memory, history, and ecology point toward tentative and experimental ways out (which are also *in*—into deeper kinship and community with human and nonhuman communities around us). As I said, these are not prescriptive steps to becoming less wasteful or consuming; rather, they are ways of seeing the world differently, or practices that promote deeper kinship. See the place you live in as bound by water rather than mapped by a grid. Write a letter to your ancestors. Learn birdsong or how to track, as a way to be constantly reminded that the world of the nonhuman surrounds us. Be at home in your body, in your bioregion. Put your hope not in the survival of the human species but in the deep earth bacteria dividing every thousand years. Excavate your psyche to find what lies in your own underlands. Walk your local river or creek. Above all, be both wide-eyed in delight at the unfolding beauty all around and clear-eyed about the legacies of destructive lifeways we have inherited.

As I continue to drive, I reflect on the significance of Dismal Swamp, and the layered meaning of the term *mossback*. One thing seems clear to me: to become a mossback means to get implicated in the mess of life. One must be comfortable with the awkward fact of having flesh, having a body with hunger and excrement. One must be willing to get entangled with the difficult histories that brought us to the present moment, and ready to proceed without knowing the right way. To be a mossback means to understand that the same economy that preys on humans also exploits nonhuman life. The extraction of timber resources from Dismal Swamp was accomplished mostly by the labor of enslaved people. And while the historical record is sparse, it indicates that mossbacks (or mossybacks) got implicated in resisting exploitation by fighting the Klan and by absconding from the Civil War.

As I ponder, the swampy landscape slowly shifts to agricultural fields in my rearview mirror. In the meantime, my imagination ferments, and a small tuft of green takes root on my back.

LIKE A MOUNTAIN

I take a few steps, stop, and inhale deeply. With each breath, the fog in my head clears a bit more. I look around. Above me are stars. Behind me, a path worn in rocks and dust fading into the deep blackness of night. Ahead—more trail, more dust, more cold. It feels like this is where I have always been. Where I will always be. My anchor to the present frays with each step, and hypoxic memories take me backward and forward through time.

I take another breath, and my mind sharpens a bit more. I am slowly moving up this great big mountain, Kilimanjaro—the roof of Africa. In this hypoxic environment, my lungs burn. My brain buzzes for lack of oxygen. Everything feels slow, fuzzy, and dreamlike. For a moment, I remember another mountain, my childhood mountain.

I am nine years old. The sun is shining overhead, and I am sitting on a bench in the corner of a field of maize in the foothills of Mount Kenya in the middle of a country smack center on the equator on the eastern edge of the great continent of Africa. Even then, the world seemed so immense.

I am in a church service. My parents are missionaries, so every Sunday we visit a different congregation in the region. Here I sit on this narrow bench, parallel with other rows of people making up this simple gathering, legs dangling in the dust, mind meandering. In a few hours, the service will be over and groups will form and enjoy hot tea with milk and stewed maize, beans, and potatoes.

But now people are singing in Kimeru, the local language, and I am looking at the triple peak of Mount Kenya peeking over clouds in the distance. I feel small and insignificant looking at this peak, and it is a strange feeling, because as a white American boy in Kenya, I am used to feeling important. Kimeru kids defer to me, and adult women defer to me, and I am used to getting what I want. *Mzungu*, they call me. It literally means "aimless" or "wanderer," and is apparently how the Bantu peoples of central Africa described the European explorers who visited the area in the eighteenth century. Now the term is used to refer to white people generally. Here I sit, a child, a wanderer, an aimless one, a white person, a kid inhabiting two cultures but at home in neither, and I stare at the rooted, enduring, ancient peaks of Mount Kenya.

Most of the people who live around Mount Kenya say that God lives on the mountain. Many of them construct their houses with doors that face the mountain as a sign of respect.

Later in my childhood, two of my friends will take me with their fathers to hike high on Mount Kenya. We will drive up to a place around seven thousand feet in elevation and park the car. Out of the back seat I and my two friends will tumble, backpacks ready with snacks and water. A trail will lead us through high grass, and soon, just as we turn a bend, we will stop in our tracks. A large cape buffalo stands in the middle of the trail, slowly chewing some of the surrounding vegetation. I will wonder if this is where I die. We will slowly walk backward, careful not to trip, until we have moved around the bend out of eyesight of the enormous creature. Then we will turn and run.

But now, in this church in a cornfield, staring at Mount Kenya, I am closer to the mountain than I have ever been. The mountain looms on the horizon. It looms over my psyche. This is my first memory of feeling a sense of the bigness of a world that has existed long before me and will continue to be long after I am gone.

I sit, staring at the mountain, my eyes a skull-door facing the mountain of God.

I start climbing again at an easy pace, my headlamp illuminating the rocks and dust a few feet ahead. My mind wanders back to the last few days on Kilimanjaro.

First, a hike through a dripping tropical rain forest on the lower slopes. My two American companions, also embarking on this exotic adventure on Mount Kilimanjaro, hike alongside me and we chat, getting to know each other. Our guides: Charlie, in his fifties, lean, hums songs to keep a slow pace for us, his clients, who breathe hard with each step as he chain-smokes his way up the trail. The other, Samuel, is a young, exuberant man, eager to talk about his wife and young children. And then, of course, the entourage of ten porters who carry the tents and kitchen from one camp to another, cook the food, draw and carry water. I hike with only a small day-pack carrying a jacket, snacks, and some water, thanks to them. Regulations require that expeditions use so many porters per person—a way to create more jobs, I'm told, though I bristle with discomfort at having such a retinue. After a long day of hiking, we camp in designated areas for climbers. When I venture out to walk around the camp, I see hundreds of tents scattered around the area.

The next day we travel through the alpine desert, with its exotic plants straining to live in the austere environment. We continue to gain elevation, and the plant life gets more and more sparse as the afternoon sun intensifies and the nights get colder.

The morning of the third day, I wake before sunrise and step out of the tent into the crisp morning air. Our camp is smaller, and there are only a few tents in the area besides those sheltering our cadre. I walk a few hundred meters and see the ground fall away. I am atop a bluff. We are now high above the clouds, but in the distance, I can see the top of neigh-boring Mount Meru erupting from the clouds. Even farther in the distance, the clouds give way, and smaller mountains push upward against the horizon. Kilimanjaro is called "the roof of Africa." I marvel at the sheer enormity of this volcanic upheaval. These peaks and ridges signify the metabolic activity of the earth: this body churning with internal heat, skin sepa-rating, drifting, folding and erupting with energy.

The ecologist Aldo Leopold gave us a lovely phrase to describe the interconnectedness of earth systems. He calls it, in his essay by the same title, "thinking like a mountain." To think like a mountain, he says, is to understand that everything is connected, and not just in an abstract way. When ranchers kill wolves, they reduce predation of deer populations. This has profound impacts on mountains, because with too many deer browsing foliage, the mountain loses the trees and plants whose roots hold the soil together. Without the wolf, the bare mountain erodes.

Thinking like a mountain also has a topological meaning. Leopold did not explore this in his short essay, but of course, as mountaineers can attest, the perspective from a mountaintop is much different than that from the valley. This is part of the draw of climbing a mountain, no matter the size. The world is different from up there in what early mountaineers called the rarified air. Before aircraft, this was the only way to get an aerial perspective of terrain. From the mountaintop, the terrestrial geometries become obvious. The landscape-level shapes of watersheds emerge. Patterns undulate across the earth, tracing the movement of water, wind, and tectonics over millennia. How can we think with a mountain-sized perspective, one that looks to the horizon, and sits in clouds, and thinks in geological epochs? Perhaps this is why so many poets and sages have gone to the mountains, for alpine visions both real and figurative. This is why we look to the high places, why we listen to prophets who come down from the mountains.

This mountain is climbed foot by tired foot, breath by gasping breath, multiplied by a million steps. In this austere air, every firing neuron, every contraction of muscle fiber comes with a great cost. Oxygen is the rate limiting factor for every movement. With every heaving breath, I am reminded of how fragile, how needy my body is. Each step, though one of many, is made with intention. There can be no thoughtless placement. A stumble or slip of the foot means lost efficiency and more oxygen demand.

My pace slows. I stop. Waves of nausea come over me. My skin tingles. I drop to my knees and vomit.

In a moment, Charlie, the mountain guide, kneels beside me and hands me a thermos of ginger tea. I turn and sit, leaning against a boulder to support my back. Slowly I sip the warm, spicy liquid. With each taste, my stomach settles a bit, and the heat radiates from my belly to the rest of my body. I feel, once again, like I have backed slowly away from death waiting round the bend in the trail. A mountain is rarely a safe place. After a few minutes, I have the strength to stand and return to my slow, methodical stepward climb.

Kilimanjaro has become a synecdoche for hierarchy. It is being consumed, and the consumers are at the top. Here, at the peak, Europeans and Americans and a smattering of others will stand, we who have the wealth it takes to get here. Most of us could not reach the top of this mountain, or this social pyramid, without the labor of Tanzanian porters, without the labor of so many nameless others who crafted the gear it took for us to reach the summit. This mountain with its social, political, and economic intricacies stands as a symbol of the historical forces that brought these people here. These are histories of the flow of resources from Africa and the Americas to Europe, histories of racial categories, histories of education and class status.

People in power tend to create a "below" so that they can stand "above" along with whomever they deem worthy.[1] This logic of hierarchy has played out across the ages but has intensified in the last five hundred years. In the European pre-Enlightenment period, as Europeans encountered more and more indigenous societies in Africa and the Americas, Africa and the Americas were cast as the "below" so that Europe could be the "above." Historian Gerald Horne sums up the strategy as "racializing and deeming inferior those not deemed to be 'white' and moving aggressively on two fronts: seizing land and enslaving willy-nilly."[2] The Church actively participated in creating this below, most effectively with a series of papal decrees authorizing the conquest of lands not occupied by Christians. According to law professor Robert A. Williams, this collection, later called the Doctrine of Discovery, "contained a mandate for Europe's subjugation of all peoples whose radical divergence from European-derived norms of right conduct signified their need for conquest and remediation."[3]

Prior to settling on this model of European superiority, imperial Christianity had already created a dichotomy of humans and nonhuman nature, which justified resource extraction without attention to the effects for the web of relations we live in. In his book *Seeing like a State*, James C. Scott traces the origins of forestry to the state's need for timber. The nascent state of Prussia needed to expand its fleet and therefore employed its scientists to catalog and measure its woodlands in order to more fully exploit them for timber.[4] Hence, forests were enclosed, surveyed, and logged without consideration of other consequences. Peasants depended on forests for fuel as well as hunting and the gathering of medicinal herbs. Where the expanding interests of the state saw value only in measurements such as the diameter at breast height of a tree—a standardized way to measure the timber value of a forest—creatures of the forest knew shelter and food, and peasants relied on forest resources as a supplement to agricultural or trade production.

In this growing logic of above and below, Europeans placed the "savages" they encountered in Africa and the Americas into the category "nature," so that as the only humans, Europeans could occupy the above in relation to the people they met in these new places. Immanuel Kant, the German philosopher whose treatises represent Enlightenment reason, serves as an example of how European supremacy came to justify the prior centuries of plunder of Africa and the Americas. His racial categorization is representative of the logic of above and below present in European thought: "Humanity exists in its greatest perfection in the white race. The yellow Indians have a smaller amount of talent. The Negroes are lower and the lowest are a part of the American peoples."[5] This allowed the justification of two things: first, the enslavement of Africans, who were not considered human, and second, the colonization of native lands, since these lands were seen as empty, as indigenous occupants were not quite human and so did not have any meaningful sovereignty.

The same European philosophical lineage that placed humans superior to the web of relations they inhabit found continuity in the establishment of a racial hierarchy with Europeans at the top. But to think like a mountain is to reject hierarchical logic. The mountain needs the wolf in order to remain a mountain. But so, too, does the wolf need the deer, and the deer relies on the mountain for its herbaceous growth. Likewise, as the scientific discipline of forestry has since come to understand (and indigenous peoples in many places have known), one cannot have a healthy forest while at the same time plundering the healthiest and most magnificent trees for timber. The forest is connected, from the squirrel that buries the acorn to the deer that browse the seedling, to the decaying nurse log feeding the next generation, to the mycelium tending growth from the underground. And because they are all connected, no part is more important than another.

Soon a faint light will appear on the horizon. My breath will be ragged and coarse, and I will use my whole body to inhale with each step, but the dawn gives me new energy. I will keep following the trail, unsure where the mountain guide is. I will start to see ice and snow, blackened with sand and dust, at the edges of the trail. At that point my body will be so deprived of oxygen I have to pause with each step to take a breath and fend off the hypoxic haze constantly threatening my brain. The risen sun will burn my face with radiation even though the rest of my body is still dulled from the cold.

Finally I will see Charlie, who has been chain-smoking his way up the mountain, even here, at nineteen thousand feet of elevation. I will feel drunk with lack of oxygen. He will beckon to me to follow him, and I will walk behind him, registering that there are other people milling about on the summit. I will be in a stupor, so finally Charlie will point me to the official summit—a worn sign, crowded around with people, that says "Uhuru peak." I will stand under the sign for a moment, and Charlie will take a picture.

As the sun rises it will continue to get warmer. I don't belong here. Even at rest, I am gasping. My brain is crying for oxygen. Does anyone belong here? Does anyone belong on any mountain? Perhaps all mountains should remain the dwelling of the gods. I will see the groups of tourists standing around, breathlessly congratulating themselves, all buoyed by the labor of hundreds of porters.

For the last several years, I've been thinking about how to escape these hierarchies and the situation we are all implicated in. It's not enough to flip the pyramid. I'm ready to pack a few essential items, leave a note, and flee to the hills. But the problem is, there is no more rough terrain. There is no place, anymore, that empire cannot reach. The entire globe has been surveyed, mapped, and partitioned.

So we must find alcoves and crags, not for escape but for a bit of respite—places where perhaps empire can reach but does completely control, because it runs out of breath. And because we cannot completely escape, we have to find a way to bring everyone along with us back to life, back to a way of being there is no need for escape from. If escape is possible, it must require both creating a community that actively rejects hierarchies and individuals willing to maintain a rough terrain of the spirit by rejecting consumerism and stories that bolster frameworks of above and below.

Across the Atlantic Ocean, a world away from Kilimanjaro, lies one such community that has been practicing escape. Since 1994, the indigenous Zapatistas in the region of Chiapas, Mexico, have been imagining and building what it means to enact a society that rejects unchecked power and

abandons hierarchies. In the absence of government aid from
the Mexican state in the region, Zapatistas have established
medical clinics and schools and created their own system to
govern themselves. Seven principles enumerate their practical
philosophy of how to work together: serve and not serve oneself; represent and not supplant; build and not destroy; pro-
pose and not impose; convince and not defeat; go below and
not above; obey and not command.[6] These principles under-
gird a political theory and practice that rejects the dualism of
above and below. The Zapatistas themselves make clear that
their model works for them, but should not merely be replicated, because context is important. In the Escuelita Zapatista
(Zapatista Little School), a program in which international
organizers learned from the Zapatista communities in 2013,
the closing plea was to return home and take the learnings "in
the way you decide to do it." The point was, "We cannot and
do not want to impose on you what to do. It is up to you to
decide."[7]

How many of us look to escape—to the mountain, the
desert commune, or a country homestead—and yet still seem
to bring with us all the worst parts of that which we try to run
from? And so it is not enough to go to the mountains for a
high-altitude perspective. We must also direct this mountain-
thinking inward, to look at the patterns of our inner landscapes, to take the bird's-eye view of our interior lives and
examine how we are shaped by the social terrain we inhabit,
the storied genealogy of our ancestral inheritance, and the
biochemical intentions of our bodies. By doing so we cultivate a sort of "rough terrain" of the spirit, a way to make it

harder for empires to completely control our desires or order our imaginations.

These things will happen soon. Shortly I will approach the top of the mountain, and I will find the guides and comrades on this expedition. But in this moment I am still climbing, and the summit is still a distant dream. I am alone and want companions on this journey. For now, there is no horizon. The fading light of my headlamp marks the edge of my view. There are only stars and cold, thin air; my fragile, contingent body; and a trail that seems forever forward and up this heaved earth, this mountain I am now a part of.

THE WATERSHED
AND THE GRID

It is fall 2015. I walk the wet streets in my neighborhood in a northern district of Portland, Oregon, watching the water collect first into trickles, then rivulets, running into the storm drains. The damp sky, so typical of the Pacific Northwest, is gray with a mist that soaks slowly. My coat is not waterproof, but I will reach the coffee shop before the rain soaks through to my shirt. I pull my hood up to better protect my face.

Watching the water run across the pavement reminds me of two maps I recently saw. One was a beautiful hand-drawn map of the city, made by Mark Lakeman. He has lived in and loved the city for many years, and he made this map based on the contours of the landscape. It is a map of the watershed, with the large Willamette River running through the middle of the page and filled with the fractal branches of tributary streams and creeks. Many of those tributaries do not exist but are his hypothesis of where water should be flowing based on the shape of the landscape.

Later I came across a map a city planner had made. This one was digital. It showed a bird's-eye view of the city grid, and the color red marked previous streams that had been paved over in the making of the city. These red former tributaries looked like blood draining into the Willamette River. This blood—these paved-over, disappeared streams—represent lost habitat, decreased water security, and increased pollutants in the Willamette and Columbia Rivers. This red stain on the map of Portland exists because of the grid overlaid across the landscape.

I first began to think about the urban grid because of Mark Lakeman. He is trained as an architect, and his imagination is city-sized. He often talks about the grid, because for so many Americans, the grid shapes the way we move across and think about the landscapes we inhabit.

The urban grid is the antithesis of the watershed. The watershed, as the fundamental unit of ecology, provides the basis for ecosystems to thrive. The grid, on the other hand, overlays an artificial geometry across the landscape and provides the political infrastructure for the extraction of resources, policing of populations, and degradation of local ecosystems. These two ways of understanding the landscapes we inhabit represent hermeneutic options—that is, methods of reading the earth.

A watershed connects all creatures in it by the common course of water through it. Species in the watershed occupy different habitats based on microclimates within the watershed, yet these creatures all still depend on the flow of water through the catchment area. By contrast, the urban grid isolates. Pavement acts as a barrier separating water from the dry soil. Existing streams are often disrupted or disappeared due to pavement. Others are buried under cement or piped into a sewer system. Streets disconnect people from their neighbors, making the space between houses dangerous due to traffic flow.

The watershed follows the natural contours of the land, whereas the urban grid levels it. As cities expand, the grid advances against native ecosystems, demolishing flora and fauna in its path and always increasing the distance between healthy ecology and human communities. In the urban grid, the dense quartering of inhabitants creates a metropolitan metabolism that outgrows the carrying capacity of the land it sits on. Thus, resources must overwhelmingly come from an external source. In the watershed, however, energy is based on the harness of light by green plants bursting from the rain-soaked soil. These plants, as the energy basis for other creatures, depend on the water cycle and the local minerals available to them.

Why are streets straight? The grid can be found across the globe, from ancient China to the pre-Columbian city of Tenochtitlan. As a planned political mechanism, the urban grid operates, according to historian Sibyl Moholy-Nagy, under the "conviction that the anonymous masses were not entitled to a free environmental choice but were to be molded by a module that was determined by an intelligence higher than their own."[1] In the West, this hallmark of city planning is attributed to Hippodamus, who developed his own birthplace of Miletus according to the grid. This geometric configuration allowed for city planning for control of the movement of goods in and out of the city, as well as managing the population. Straight streets allow military or police personnel a long line of sight and effective movement from one location to another. As James C. Scott notes, observing the correlation between gridded streets and municipal authority, "The elective affinity between a strong state and a uniformly laid out city is obvious."[2] Sociologist Lewis Mumford elaborates how the grid functioned for imperial designs: "The very weakness of the [grid] plan—its indifference to the contours of the land, to springs, rivers, shore lines, clumps of trees—only made it that much more admirable in providing a minimum basis of order on a site that colonists would not, for long, have the means to fully exploit. Within the shortest possible time, everything was brought under control."[3]

While the Greeks invented the grid in the Mediterranean, the Romans perfected it for just the sort of colonization that Mumford describes. The Roman castrum, a military encampment, used a grid layout that led to a uniformity perfect for a traveling military. With this standard camp plan, soldiers always knew how to navigate the large base regardless of where it was located. A newly arrived soldier could easily procure rations, find a commanding officer, or seek a bed. As the Roman military conquered more land, military encampments easily and naturally became colonies, already planned according to Roman taste, whereas most conquered towns were a winding maze of streets that had developed over time. Since retired soldiers often populated colonies, the castrum-based layout could be quickly recognized and navigated by these citizens.

The grid plan was used throughout the centuries as a means of managing people and nature, but its ultimate iteration as a colonization tool came about when it was expanded by the newly formed United States in 1785. The Land Ordinance of 1785 stipulated that the land of Ohio and westward be divided into a grid that could be subdivided from the level of county down to individual lots. Moholy-Nagy calls this act the full-circle "rebirth of Roman colonialism," which converted land from a life-giving source to a speculative commodity.[4]

As Euro-American settlers pushed west, the grid followed, allowing settlers to stake out homestead claims. However, in the arid lands west of the 100th meridian—approximately halfway through Kansas—homesteading became increasingly difficult. Annual evaporation approached or surpassed annual rainfall, making traditional agriculture unfeasible without irrigation. Geologist John Wesley Powell predicted this problem with the traditional homesteading pattern of settlement and hence proposed an alternative to the grid: he suggested creating "watershed commonwealths," organized by a nested pattern of watersheds, instead of partitioning western lands according to the Land Ordinance of 1785. These watershed commonwealths would ensure that residents have decisive control over their own scarce water, allowing them to mitigate their own water conflicts. Further, because the settlers of these commonwealths would have to fund and manage their own water resources, the population of the western lands would remain low enough to be supported by the limited water supply. Powell's vision was unpopular. Congress wanted to retain rights to the timber and mining resources; developers feared that the commonwealth idea would slow expansion in the West; homesteaders did not want to wait for the land to be properly surveyed and organized into watershed districts. The grid won out over the watershed.

Ultimately, three-quarters of the United States came under the gridiron plan. Thus, the geometric layout—which ignores the contours of land, the aspects of weather, and especially the flow of water in the watershed—was overlaid across an entire continent. According to Mumford, the gridiron was capitalism writ large onto the landscape: "On strictly commercial principles, the gridiron plan answered, as no other plans did, the shifting values, the accelerated expansion, the multiplying population, required by the capitalist regime."[5]

In 1881, Alice Fletcher went to live with the Omaha in Nebraska. She had extensive experience as an anthropologist, having studied archaeology with Francis Putnam at Harvard University. Her time with the Omaha Sioux fostered one of her many tribal relationships; she also worked with the Nez Perce in Idaho and the Miwok in California. Fletcher's close relationship with Francis La Flesche, the first Native American ethnologist, represented her personal as well as professional interest in Native Americans. However, although she admired many of the Indians she lived and worked with, Fletcher still thought white civilization superior. She feared that native tribes would lose their lands and lobbied Congress to apportion Omaha lands to individuals so that the tribal lands could not be ceded. She supervised the allotment with the assistance of La Flesche, and this experience led her to cowrite the Dawes Act of 1887, leading to the survey and allotment of Indian lands.

Under the Dawes Act, the gridiron plan was extended even into the territory of the reservations given to American Indian tribes. The act called for plotting and partitioning tribally held lands (excluding a few Native American groups, among them what were then called the Five Civilized Tribes—the nations of the Cherokee, Chickasaw, Choctaw, Creek, and Seminole) into a grid plan similar to that established by the Land Ordinance of 1785. Bringing tribal land under the gridiron plan commoditized Indian land into individual holdings, dividing communal land tenure and effectively breaking tribal government.

Dawes believed this move would ultimately be helpful to the Indian tribes. In a speech about the Cherokee he notes, "They have no selfishness, which is the bottom of civilization. Till this people will consent to give up their lands, and divide them among their citizens . . . they will not make much more progress."[6]

Where Dawes was either ignorant or naive, his contemporary, Thomas Morgan, the commissioner of Indian Affairs, was simply brutal. In his 1889 annual report, he expressed the true intent of federal policy: "The Indians must conform to the white man's ways, peaceably if they will, forcibly if they must. They must adjust themselves to their environment and conform their mode of living substantially to our civilization. This civilization may not be the best possible, but it is the best the Indians can get. They cannot escape it and must either conform to it or be crushed by it."[7]

By the early twentieth century, 92 million acres of Indian lands were lost due to this plan. The grid thus arose from an imperial practice utilized in specific colonies in Western civilization to become a hegemonic tool of empire the United States employed in genocide and land appropriation.

Water and civilizations are inextricably linked. All major settlements must lie close to a water source for the daily needs of citizenry. In southern Mesopotamia, where rainfall was eight inches or less, all cities were located on the major rivers of the Tigris and the Euphrates. Thus, concurrent with the growth of urbanization in the region was the need to harness water for the agriculture necessary to support civilization. Urban attempts to control water ultimately failed, however, for multiple reasons.

The practice of irrigation was a major contributing factor to the downfall of early Mesopotamian civilization. This irrigation took the form of many canals extending throughout the region, which over time drastically changed the landscape by the process of desertification and salinization. Irrigation precipitates salinization, particularly in arid regions; added water raises the water table, bringing underground minerals to the surface. As the water is used by plants or evaporates, it leaves behind the salts. In Mesopotamia, there is not enough rainfall to leach the salts, and over time these minerals accumulate to increase soil salinity and damage crop yield. Salting of the land caused crop failure, as documented in the Atrahasis epic, a nineteenth-century BCE Akkadian tale from Mesopotamia: "The black fields became white, the broad plains choked with salt."[8] The salinization of soil over time shifted the trend in growing wheat to the more salt-tolerant barley.

Due to its scarcity, water became a resource many kingdoms battled over to control. When the third-millennium kingdoms of Girsu and Umma had conflict, Umma, located higher on the watershed, blocked canals and changed watercourses in order to cripple Girsu's water availability. Later the powerful king of Babylon, Hammurabi, manipulated water flows in a conflict with Eshnunna, a rival city-state. Royal records claim that he inundated the city by redirecting water to "destroy Eshnunna with a great flood." More than a thousand years after Hammurabi, the Neo-Babylonian empire itself fell as a result of water engineering. In his *Histories* Herodotus records that Cyrus breached the city by diverting some of the Euphrates so that his army could enter the city through the riverbank.

Finally, the natural meandering pattern of the rivers, extensive due to the geography of the plain, shifted settlement patterns and caused extensive problems for many cities. A classic example comes from the Meander River, the source of our English word *meandering*. The natural movement of the river was exacerbated by sedimentation due to deforestation up the watershed, such that the mouth of the river moved several miles from the port city of Priene. In Babylon, the Euphrates historically divided the heart of the city but now cuts through the city's western half. This change in course has been attributed by some to Nebuchadnezzar's palace, built so close to the riverbank as to modify the leeway of floods.

Philosopher Jacques Ellul notes that the first city mentioned in the Torah, built by Cain, was called *Enoch*, meaning "inaugurate" or "initiate."[9] The earth was not enough, so a new world order had to be inaugurated. Similarly, Babylon symbolizes the triumph of the city itself over nature, with the grid impressed on the landscape as the epitome of the human will over natural process. By the time of the Neo-Babylonian empire, the region was quite an urban society. Archaeologists have found that more than half of the inhabited areas dated to this time lived in cities of ten thousand inhabitants or more. Anthropologist Robert McCormick Adams regards the concentration of population in Ancient Mesopotamia as a "hypertrophic, 'unnatural' condition for an agricultural civilization with preindustrial transport technology."[10] This is partly why Mesopotamian kingdoms depended on a politics of extraction. As theologian Hans Barstad remarks: "The Neo-Babylonian empire represented a highly developed civilization, with an advanced political and economic structure . . . Having no natural resources of its own, the whole existence of the empire depended entirely upon the import of materials like metals, stone, and timber, and all sorts of food and luxury items."[11]

From street level, what could be seen within the city—other than the line of sight down the street and the accompanying buildings—would have been the ziggurat, the temple of Marduk, patron god of the city. A yearly procession led the statue of Marduk from the temple sanctuary through the streets of the city and far outside the walls into the uncultivated steppe, and this ritual, according to Marc Van De Mieroop, would "turn the whole countryside into sacred landscape."[12] The Babylonian epic *Enuma Elish* records Marduk slaying Tiamat, primordial goddess of water and chaos, in order to fashion from her corpse the world, with humans dwelling in it to serve the gods. The symbolism is clear: Babylon's patron deity overcomes primordial nature by violence. As Cain sought to reinaugurate the world with the first city, as Marduk conquers chaos, so the city renders nature servile and domesticated. This ceremony represented the city as the remaking of the world by humans, writ onto the landscape with the grid in juxtaposition to the complex, mosaic landscape of the alluvial plain.

Babylon stands in a long line of imperial regimes that used the grid pattern to effect rule over a populace. Much of the city was laid out roughly in what city planners call an orthogonal pattern, in which streets intersect at approximately right angles. This grid was part of an overall plan that sought to emphasize the role of the city in imposing order on a chaotic world. Van De Mieroop tells us that "the role of the city as an organizing principle in the universe was also the role of its god Marduk, the one who brings order to the universe." He elaborates, "Both god and city were forces of order in a world of chaos."[13]

This betrays a symbolic division between human and nature, city and countryside, that has only intensified in the subsequent centuries. The grid is a psychological barrier, enclosing not only the landscape but also our minds. Eco-philosopher David Abram reminds us:

> Caught up in a mass of abstractions, our attention hypnotized
> by a host of human-made technologies that only reflect us
> back to ourselves, it is all too easy for us to forget our carnal
> inheritance in a more-than-human matrix of sensations and
> sensibilities. Our bodies have formed themselves in delicate
> reciprocity with the manifold textures, sounds, and shapes of
> an animate earth—our eyes have evolved in subtle interaction
> with other eyes, as our ears are attuned by their very structure
> to the howling of wolves and the honking of geese. To shut
> ourselves off from these other voices, to continue by our
> lifestyles to condemn these other sensibilities to the oblivion
> of extinction, is to rob our own senses of their integrity, and

to rob our minds of their coherence. We are human only in
contact, and conviviality, with what is not human.[14]

In southeastern England, the modern city of Colchester lies
atop the ruins of a first-century Roman colonia. This colony
was established by Emperor Claudius, who, after his conquest
of England, established this city by expanding a traditional
castrum in the center of the native town of Camulodunon.
The site, newly named Camulodunum, became the main
Roman outpost in the region—and as a colonia, its citizens
had Roman citizenship. Soon it boasted Roman temples and
theaters. Retired soldiers who settled in the city were tasked
with Romanizing the Britons as well as defending the city
against the threat of rebels in the countryside.

An archaeological discovery in Turkey sheds light on how
the Britons were perceived by Rome. Excavations in the
ancient Roman city of Aphrodisias have uncovered, among
other items, a relief of Claudius. This relief in the temple
shows the emperor framing the top of the sculpture, nude,
with the exception of a helmet on his head and a cape bil-
lowing behind him. On the ground below him lies a woman,
right breast bared, hips on the ground, and torso raised. The
male is grabbing her head with his left hand, and appears to
be violently holding it up; his right arm is raised, and, though
the relief is broken, appears to have been wielding a sword.
The figures are identified as the Emperor Claudius and the
woman as the nation of Britannia, Rome's most significant
exploit during his reign.

The logic of Roman empire is quite explicit in this rendering. As men dominate women, so does Claudius, as *pater*

patriae—father of the fatherland—dominate the nations (who are feminized). This logic incorporates the castrum, which is the angular geometry of dominance inflicted on the landscape. Moreover, in keeping with Roman tradition since Augustus, the deification of the emperor was displayed in the colony with a temple dedicated to the cult of Claudius. This temple was an additional insult, built at the expense of and with the labor of the local Britons.

Roman settlers embodied the same demeanor toward Britons that they saw modeled by Claudius and Rome. The historian Tacitus records the grievances inflicted by military veterans: "These new settlers in the colony of Camulodunum drove people out of their houses, ejected them from their farms, called them captives and slaves."[15]

For other Britons, the sculpture described above became more than symbolic. When Prasutagas, client king of Britain, died, his wife Boudicca was flogged and his daughters raped by Roman soldiers. Moreover, Rome seemed to see the death of Prasutagas as an opportunity to consolidate power in the region: they confiscated the property of Prasutagas and demanded the return of loans given to wealthy Britons with a large interest fee attached. Boudicca subsequently led a revolt, gathering her own people, the Iceni, and allying with the Trinovantes, the local tribe in the countryside around Camulodunum, who despised the Roman colony and its settlers.

We know of Boudicca and the uprising through the accounts of two historians, Tacitus and Cassius Dio, both of whom were Romans. They describe Boudicca as tall and fierce, with long tawny hair, wearing a tunic and cloak. Indeed, she is described as a warrior and a diviner, who took a hare from her cloak before battle to interpret victory. She was the chosen leader of the rebellion and identified herself not as an elite but as a Briton who, like her comrades, was oppressed by Rome. Tacitus records her speech: "It is not as a woman descended from noble ancestry, but as one of the people that I am avenging lost freedom, my scourged body, the outraged chastity of my daughters."[16]

While the Roman governor Suetonius was away from Camulodunum on a military campaign, the insurgents took the opportunity to attack. They vastly outnumbered the Roman soldiers left behind, and in two days they took the city. Boudicca and her forces wasted no time in dismantling the temple to Claudius, razing the colony with the castrum at its center, and burning it to the ground. They went on to attack three more Roman towns in the province.

Meanwhile, Suetonius got word of the uprising and gathered his forces. The exact location of the meeting of the armies is unknown, but Tacitus and Dio both provide records of Boudicca's speech. Before Boudicca led her warriors into battle, she reminded them that by virtue of their relationship to their landscape, they had more security than the Romans:

They require shade and covering, they require kneaded bread and wine and oil, and if any of these things fails them, they perish; for us, on the other hand, any grass or root serves as bread, the juice of any plant as oil, any water as wine, any tree as a house. Furthermore, this region is familiar to us and is our ally, but to them it is unknown and hostile. As for the rivers, we swim them naked, whereas they do not cross them easily even with boats. Let us, therefore, go against them trusting

boldly to good fortune. Let us show them that they are hares
and foxes trying to rule over dogs and wolves.[17]

This speech represents the contrasting visions of life that met
on the battlefield that day. Her words show the fundamental
difference between the watershed and the grid—the former
is a site of relationship and the economic ecology of mutual
aid, whereas the latter is the site of conflict and extraction. For
Rome the landscape was merely another space to be dominated
after the conquer of foreign feminized bodies. Just as Claudius
presumed to vanquish the feminized province of Britannia, so
the Roman castrum conquered the British landscape, imposing a grid of control over people and territory. The urban grid
was a way to make familiar the unknown countryside. But
Boudicca and her kin did not need the geometry of the grid,
because they had a long-standing relationship to the region.

The Latin language has multiple connotations for the word *rivalis*, the source of our modern word *rival.* The original meaning
of the word is "of or belonging to a brook." The second, derived
from the first, is "neighbors," or "those who share the same
brook." One can imagine how that meaning would have developed, as landowning Romans who lived on opposite sides of a
stream or brook would be neighbors and sometimes rivals over
water. This usage of the term led to the third meaning, "one
who shares the same mistress," or a competitor in love.

    Rivers feature often within Roman history as symbols of
rivalry and competition. Julius Caesar famously crossed the
Rubicon River, leading to civil war. Before that, his crossing
of the Rhine proved the engineering prowess of the military

and led to the defeat of the Gauls. Later, in the fourth century CE, another civil war erupted between Constantine and Maxentius. The conflict came to a head at the banks of the Tiber River. Indeed, the founding myth of Romulus and Remus features this conflict between belonging and competition. The infant brothers, according to Plutarch, were saved from slaughter by being placed in a trough next to a river. This river swelled over its banks, carrying the brothers safely to a place where they were found and nurtured by a she-wolf. Later, during the founding of the city of Rome, these two brothers who shared that river journey became rivals, and Romulus succeeded in killing Remus.

The word *rivalis* betrays the Roman understanding of water as cleaver of relationship. For the Romans, two farm steads along opposite sides of a river would inevitably clash over water usage. They saw neighbors as riven by the river. But this is quite opposite the ecological understanding of rivers. In the fundamental ecological unit of the watershed, the river is a synecdoche for the entire landscape united by water flowing across it. The two sides of the river are part of a larger whole, amalgamated by gravity's pull and water's life-giving properties. The landscape is not riven, and neighbors need not be rivals. James Ransom, a member of the Wolf clan of the Mohawk Nation and an environmental engineer, discusses how a seventeenth-century treaty belt, the Kaswentha, offers guidance for restoration of both riverine waterways as well as settler-indigenous relations:

> The Treaty Belt is made of two rows of purple wampum beads,
> and these two rows have the spirit of the Haudenosaunee

and the Dutch . . . The two purple rows depict two vessels travelling down a river. One, a birch-bark canoe, is for the Haudenosaunee and contains our laws, customs, and way of life. The other, a ship, is for the Dutch and contains their laws, customs, and way of life. The purpose of the Treaty is to recognize that each People is to travel down this river together, side-by-side but each in their own vessel . . . The treaty recognizes that the Haudenosaunee and Dutch share the same river, the river of life. We are to help each other, from time to time, as we travel this river together. We are to take care of this river as all of our survival depends on a healthy river.[18]

Where the Romans saw only division, the Haudenosaunee found a possibility of friendship. The stream symbolizes connectedness. To use my friend Jonathan McRay's lovely phrase, "The river is reconciliation." This is represented by Boudicca's relationship to the river, not as a divide to be carefully crossed but as a body to swim naked in, connoting intimacy, knowledge, and trust. If the grid testifies to the attempt to control nature, Boudicca's speech is a counter-testimony that humans live not by roads, bricks, and mortar but, rather, by those fleeting photons captured by the chlorophyll in grass and every green plant. The web of life in the watershed will endure beyond the grid.

AFTER APOCALYPSE

The summer of 2012 was hot in the Midwest. By the fourth week of temperatures above ninety degrees Fahrenheit, and more than two months without rain, the grass was brown and many of our crops in northeastern Indiana were not faring much better.

I lived on a twenty-six-acre farm, three acres of which my friends and I were homesteading and vegetable gardening. Our farm—Bluefield Farm, named after the abundant chicory, with its blue blossoms—was an oasis in the middle of an industrial agriculture desert. The surrounding landscape was filled with acres of corn and soybean. Most of the farm lay pastured with organic hay, but we planted market gardens on about one and a half acres of the land.

The work was hard but rewarding. Gardens require thoughtful soil preparation—compost or manure ensure proper nutrition for the plants, and manual tillage loosens the soil so that roots can take hold and take up crucial minerals; unlike plowing, it does so without killing beneficial worms and fungal threads. Hand tillage and planting even two acres can be backbreaking, but shared labor lightened the work and even made it enjoyable. Mentors helped us to know when to start seeds and how and when to transplant, and offered tips and strategies for dealing with insects and weeds without utilizing chemicals. Late-night research provided information on companion and succession planting, to negotiate plant tolerance and space. And always, the gardens humbled us with our amateur knowledge of how to grow enough to feed ourselves with a margin of extra.

The contrast between our farm and the surrounding agricultural practices was evident on a daily basis. Our small-scale gardens were planted with seedlings before the surrounding fields were dry enough for the tractors to till. Even in the heat and drought of 2012, we had some crops that survived. The diversity of our planting plan meant that although some of our vegetables did not tolerate the hot, dry weather, others did. Surrounding us, though, were thousands of acres of soybean and corn that desiccated into brown stalks without the water they needed. The scale of those farms of hundreds or even thousands of acres of monoculture meant that weather extremes had a devastating effect on the crop yield.

But it was an event that summer—a disaster—that truly marked the difference between industrial food production and the small-scale agroecology we practiced on Bluefield Farm. A quarter mile up the road was another kind of farm: a chicken farm, but more properly just a collection of large industrial buildings. This was an egg production facility, alleged to provide all the eggs for all the stores of a large grocery chain east of the Mississippi. I believed this to be true, because it consisted of four buildings, each a quarter mile long and one hundred yards wide. The factory boasted of 2 million hens, each housed in a cage constructed such that the daily egg born of their bodies was moved via a conveyor belt to be collected, cleaned, bleached, and packaged. Production was mechanized to facilitate as little human intervention as possible, but workers were still needed for various tasks. One of the inauspicious duties was the daily chore of collecting dead birds from their cages and throwing them out.

I was in town one scorching day when I heard the news from one of the locals—the giant fans, big as airplane engines, just couldn't keep up with the heat. Those big buildings had become giant ovens, and three hundred thousand chickens had died from hyperthermia.

When I got home from town, I rushed over to our small chicken coop, constructed of leftover odds and ends of wood and tin nailed onto a frame of two by fours. Our ten hens were fine, pecking away at the occasional insect and fussing about as they generally did under the shade of a tree. For the rest of the day, though, I could hear the commotion of large machinery in the distance. I was told that they buried the dead chickens—all three hundred thousand—in a massive heap of feathers, flesh, and bones.

That event felt like an apocalypse. I did not fully realize at the time that this land had already experienced a massive apocalypse brought on by settlers from the United States, eager for new land to clear and farm. That apocalypse started with the displacement of native people and continues to this day in the monocultural miles of corn and soy.

A mere fifty miles by road from Bluefield Farm, the Potawatomi Trail of Death began.[1] On November 13, 1838, Father Joseph Petit, a Jesuit priest, wrote the following description of the caravan to Bishop Bruté:

> The order of the march was as follows: the United States
> flag, carried by a dragoon (soldier); then one of the principal
> officers, next the staff baggage carts, then the carriage, which
> during the whole trip was kept for the use of the Indian chiefs;
> then one or two chiefs on horseback led a line of 250 or 300
> horses ridden by men, women, children in single file, after the
> manner of savages. On the flanks of the line at equal distance
> from each other were the dragoons and volunteers, hastening
> the stragglers, often with severe gestures and bitter words.
> After this cavalry came a file of 40 baggage wagons filled with
> luggage and Indians. The sick were lying in them, rudely jolted,
> under a canvas that, far from protecting them from the dust
> and heat, only deprived them of air, for they were as if buried
> under this burning canopy—several died thus.[2]

For the year prior, Petit had been a missionary to the Potawatomi band near Fort Wayne, Indiana. He had been away from Twin Lakes, Indiana, when the Potawatomi Trail of Death began, but had petitioned his superior so that he could join the villagers with whom he had become acquainted. By the time he was able to join the forcibly displaced Potawatomi, many had already fallen ill.

The US government had made multiple attempts to assimilate the Potawatomis. President Jefferson, ever the champion of the farm, expressed his hope to integrate the tribe into European ways of farming. In a letter to Chiefs Little Turtle and Five Medals, he relayed the following: "We shall with pleasure see your people become disposed to cultivate the earth, to raise heards [*sic*] of useful animals, and to spin and weave for their food and clothing."[3]

A few chiefs had expressed interest in learning settler agriculture, but the overwhelming majority of Potawatomi had no interest in the hard lifestyle. Attempts by Quakers to create a model farm to teach the Potawatomi failed; the few men who started to assist with farmwork soon lost interest, and the leader of the effort, a man by the name of Phillip Dennis, soon gave up.

While the Potawatomi did assimilate somewhat by adopting some of the textiles and goods that Americans sold, they maintained their own traditional lifeways. They continued to live in the wigwam-style houses common to the region, and planted small gardens of corn, beans, and squash in the summer, supplementing their diet with hunting in the winter. Officials and missionaries agreed that the tribe had not made strides toward "white civilization." They "adhered with tenacity to the manners of their forefathers while everything around them has changed," according to one report.[4]

Potawatomi lands were ceded piecemeal over a quarter century, starting in 1816. This process was complicated by the multiple Potawatomi chiefs involved, as well as the many federal agencies and agents. Population pressure from settlers arriving from the east caused problems for the Potawatomi traditional lifestyle. Overhunting and overtrapping by fur traders and settlers had reduced the deer herds and small game, which the natives depended on for winter food. Settlers were happy to hunt in Potawatomi lands but got angry when the Indians encroached on their farms and settlements.

There is a phrase for what happened in the Midwest, as in so many places across North America. "Settler colonialism" does not fly smoothly out of the lips. It rattles in the mouth and rakes the tongue across the teeth. Yet it is the best jargon we have to speak with brevity about a process that took a few centuries.

Settler colonialism is the force behind indigenous genocide. As Potawatomi scholar Kyle Powhys White explains, settler colonialism is directly related to ecology. Colonization generally follows one of two paths: keep the indigenous way of life intact and extract resources from its system, or remake the landscape into one that is similar to the colonizing homeland. In North America, settlers created a narrative of the forest ecosystems of the eastern woodlands as unmanaged. This created a justification for colonization: because native people were seen as not stewarding the land, European settlers were obliged to conquer nature and make it productive. This narrative erased indigenous lifeways and ecological knowledge.

The settler legends of Paul Bunyan, lumberjack of the Great Lakes woodlands, represent this glorification of taming the wild forest. Paul Bunyan is a larger-than-life figure, famed for his speed at cutting down trees. With his accomplice, a similarly caricatured big blue ox, he rambles about the woods chopping down trees and otherwise manifesting power over natural forces like cold winters and wild animals. Paul Bunyan is a settler hero. He gazes upon a wooded landscape and sees timber. He clear-cuts the way for the settler ecology of annual crops—fields of grains.

What were seen as unproductive, pristine forests were actually tended landscapes that provided for Native American life. Nut-bearing trees provided staple calories. Open meadows provided browse for deer and other game animals. A wide range of encouraged herbs and woody perennials provided for basketry, medicine, and other crafts. Even tribes that were primarily farmers were not recognized as such, since their farms did not look like those of the European settlers. Because of this, Native Americans were killed, displaced, or otherwise marginalized, and at the same time their native ecosystems deforested and cleared for European-style farms. Thus, indigenous genocide and ecocide went hand in hand.

By 1826 the Potawatomi already felt the ecological effects of settlers in their landscape. A Potawatomi chief, Awbanawben, said,

You said we could not stay here. We would perish. But what
will perish[?] But what will destroy us[?] It is yourselves
destroying us . . . You trampled on our soil, and drove it
away. Before you came, the game was plenty, but you drove it
away . . . You point to a country for us in the west, where there
is game . . . but the Great Spirit has made and put men there
who have a right to that game and it is not ours.[5]

A conflict in LaSalle County, Illinois, was paradigmatic of settler-indigenous relations in the area. A man named William Davis set up a mill and a blacksmith shop on Indian Creek. He dammed the creek to power the mill, which prevented fish from swimming upstream, where a village of Potawatomis lived. This disregard of their food supply angered the villagers, and tensions grew. Davis refused to give in despite being warned by other Potawatomi chiefs who attempted to intervene, and he gathered more settler families around his homestead in an effort to dig in. Eventually, a group of forty Potawatomi attacked the settlement, killing Davis and other men and capturing some women and children.

American settlers continued to pour into the region. Even where Potawatomi had agreed to cede land or allow settlement, land was occupied and cleared for farming so quickly that Chief Metea complained, "The plowshare is driven through our tents before we have time to carry out our goods and seek another habitation."[6] When new lands were opened for settlement after sale or treaty, often the land-hungry farmers would take up residence before surveyors had properly demarcated the sections belonging to Potawatomi and those open for settlers, creating tension and confusion.

Growing tensions and rising populations of settlers added to the "Indian problem." By the time President Jackson had signed the Indian Removal Act in 1830, the Potawatomi had already sold much of their land, and had lost much of the land community that gave them food, medicine, and shelter, due to the continual encroachment of white settler farms. The Indian Removal Act stipulated that the relocation of tribes would be voluntary and that they would move to land west of the Mississippi.

In 1836, Abel Pepper, commissioned to attempt to purchase the remaining reservation lands in Indiana, compiled a group of dubious Potawatomi leaders he called "the Chiefs warriors, and headmen of the Patawattamies of the Wabash." Although this group had little claim over the land or recognition from the villagers, the Senate recognized the treaty as valid and ratified it. Chief Menominee, one of the leaders who refused to sign or acknowledge the treaty, gave the following charge, worth quoting in full:

> The president does not know the truth. He, like me, has been imposed upon. He does not know that you made my young chiefs drunk and got their consent and pretended to get mine . . . He would not drive me from my home and the graves of my tribe, and my children, who have gone to the Great Spirit, nor allow you to tell me that your braves will take me, tied like a dog . . . The President is just, but he listens to the words of young chiefs who have lied; and when he knows the truth, he will leave me to my own. I have not sold my lands. I will not sell them. I have not signed any treaty, and will not sign any. I am not going to leave my lands.[7]

But the president was not just. White settlers had already been promised the lands around Twin Lakes, Indiana, that Menominee refused to cede. Squatters came, intent on taking the best land before the crowds, and a Potawatomi party burned a squatter's hut, leading to retaliation from settlers, who then burned down a dozen Indian homes.

Pepper requested military assistance, and Senator John Tipton gathered one hundred volunteers for a militia to remove the remaining Potawatomi to land in Kansas. On August 30, 1838, Tipton had the remaining villagers gather, and his militia surrounded the villagers and forced them to enroll for removal, giving them five days to gather their things. Five days later, the march began. Still Menominee would not leave the village, so he was forced at gunpoint to go, and was placed under arrest with two other chiefs who also resisted.

The march to the Osage River in Kansas, more than six hundred miles away, began on September 4, 1838, and concluded sixty-one days later. Of the forty-two people who died during the march, twenty-eight were children. Petit survived the march, and much of what we know is recorded in his journal.

In 1891, Oscar Wilde wrote a play elaborating on the story of the beheading of John the Baptist. The biblical account simply notes a dancer, the daughter of Herodias, who danced before King Herod and his friends. The dance was so remarkable that Herod promised her anything she wanted, up to half his kingdom, yet what she requested—after consulting her mother—was the head of John the Baptist on a platter. Her mother had her own grudge against the prophet John, who had criticized her for marital machinations. Salome, unnamed in the biblical account but known by historical sources, danced her way into the center of a conflict between prophet and power.

This short story inspired Wilde's play *Salome and the Seven Veils*. Wilde deepened the story by adding the motif of the seven veils. The seven veils, a departure from the biblical story, allude to the myth of the descent of Inanna. This Ancient Sumerian deity was understood to be the goddess of fertility. She is a character in many of the myths, and one of the most famous is the account of her journey to the underworld of the dead. In the story, Inanna encounters seven gates, and at each she must remove a garment, until she stands naked at the throne of the goddess of the underworld, her sister Ereshkigal. For Wilde, the veils of Salome symbolize this movement toward the deathly realm. With the removal of each veil, death dances closer.

French writer Alphonse Allais took the story's death allegory even further. In his rendering, Salome removes the veils accompanied by the lusty cries of Herod. "Go on, go on," he says. Yet when the last veil falls, he continues to shout for more. Salome complies by ripping the skin from her body. And still Herod says, "Go on," so she continues to flay fascia with her fingernails, layer by visceral layer, until nothing is left but bone.

Apocalypse means "unveiling." Originally the word referred to the lifting of a bride's veil at a wedding, but it has since taken on symbolic meaning. Popular usage makes apocalypse about the end of the world.

In apocalypse, everything hidden will be revealed. But the face underneath the veil is not always good. Sometimes the apocalypse is the lover who tells you they are leaving. Sometimes it is the cold calm of a doctor relaying a cancer diagnosis. Occasionally unveiling is beautiful, like the brief moment near dusk when the light slants through the pines and the woods reveal a momentary beauty previously unknown. But mostly apocalypse pulls back the social fabric of cloth and skin to show the structural bones underneath.

For writers in the ancient genre called apocalyptic, the revealing is about power, history, and hope. Their prophetic imaginations pull back the veil on empires like Babylon and Rome to expose a view from the underbelly. This kind of apocalypse is not personal. It is as big as the arc of history. The subject is not people but powers. Kings become beasts, militaries their horns. Politics play out in the imaginal realm as

the beasts vie for control. Within this imaginal realm, apocalyptic writing discloses the dreams of the disempowered.
An end to oppression approaches. So many heads of so many
beasts become decapitated. Magical scrolls foretell future vin-
dication. Trumpets blast sounds of triumph. Lakes of fire and
glittering cities signify the fate, respectively, of the damned
and the delivered.

Just because apocalyptic writing has creative imagery does
not mean that it is fanciful. Apocalypse is an exercise of what
anthropologist David Graeber calls "imaginative counterpower," which is to say, it helps the oppressed name the powers that seem to control their lives, as well as to imagine an
end to these powers.[8] As oral stories, they inspire the hearer.
As texts, they show the reader a view from the belly of history,
from the people with a knife to their throats as the military
raids the coffers and the granaries.

And apocalypse always shows the skeletons. In the midst of
kings shouting with lust, "Go on"—more power, more money,
ever more consolidation of resources—apocalypse pulls back
the flesh and fascia to show the bone-dead trajectory of their
desire.

The book of Daniel is one such apocalyptic text, written
during the Antiochean rule of Palestine to aid the imagination of an occupied people. It reflects the memory of Hebrew
people exiled and taken to Babylon and thus operates in code:
"We have been under the thumb of other rulers before," the
story seems to say, "and managed to find a way then, so we can
do the same now."

In the first chapter, the author sets the tone for the book
in portraying Daniel and his friends as ones who—despite

being captive to the empire—attempt to live faithfully to their indigenous ways within it. The story introduces Daniel and friends as intelligent members of Jerusalem's elite taken into service for the king. This assimilation of members of the elite is an important imperial strategy: in the same way that the urban grid represents a control measure for civilians, putting the social elite at the king's table essentially puts them under his thumb.

In the king's service, Daniel and his friends were given Babylonian names. This renaming reveals how their lives were meant to be reshaped according to the priorities of Babylon. Just as later nation-states developed surnames in order to track and tax populations, so the renaming of newly acquired servants is a measure of the degree to which Babylon claimed authority over the lives of the political prisoners.

The first narrative of these Jewish captives centers around food. Like other high-ranking captives, these friends were offered food from the king's table. Daniel's refusal of the king's food constitutes the crux of the story. *Patbag*, the word at issue here, is the allotted meal taken from the royal coffers to meet the needs of his courtiers. Most interpreters take this refusal to be a religious one—Jews in antiquity often maintained their ethnic and religious distinction vis-à-vis food purity by observing dietary rules. In diasporic communities, food connects people to their culture. Even modern food sovereignty movements advocate for culturally appropriate food. An overlooked area of this issue, however, is that the royal court system depended on an empire that extracted goods from the margins of empire to benefit the center. As David Vanderhooft, a scholar of the Ancient Near East, notes, wresting resources from the conquered periphery to the king's palace was commonplace: "The procedure of funneling resources from the subject populations to the heartland through seizure and exaction was no less important to the Babylonians as it had been to the Assyrians . . . Nebuchadnezzar campaigned almost yearly in the west, in part to insure order, but also to fill the royal coffers."[9]

The king's table would certainly be maintained by such imperial campaigns; meat and wine would be sourced from tribute from conquered nations, meat being transportable as livestock, and wine as an imperishable good that could travel distance without spoiling. Meanwhile, the average urban dweller in Babylon had a diet that was more likely grain-based, dependent on cereals transported from the surrounding countryside. Babylon's "foodprint," according to one catalog of grain imports, consisted of an area extending from Sippa in the north to Sealand in the south, a length of 186 miles of irrigated land.[10] By contrast, perishable vegetables do not travel well and thus would have to be grown nearby.

Daniel's requested diet of vegetables and water represents an alternative to the extractive economy of empire in favor of local fare that could not be stolen from distant places. The refusal of the king's table food, therefore, can be read not just as a dietary preference but also as an act of defiance. If acceptance of the king's food symbolized political allegiance, the alternative diet was an implicit rejection of the king. "We will not nourish our bodies with your pillage," they seemed to say. The four friends might have to live in the king's court, but they would find ways to resist the politics of plunder epitomized by the *patbag*.

Once the snow melted on the Indiana roads, I would often ride my bike from our farm to town. I learned quickly, however, that early summer was the spraying time. I pedaled past acres of corn and soybean down the straight county roads. When the tractors were out, pulling large tanks labeled "anhydrous ammonia," I had to hope the wind was blowing the fumes away from the road. When the breeze was not in my favor, I did my best to pedal furiously, holding my breath and hoping I could pass the cloud without inhaling too much of it. At other times, the chemical applicants were not labeled, or were dropped by prop plane, so I could not know what noxious admixtures made it into my lungs. These chemicals, fertilizers, herbicides, and pesticides—so crucial to industrial agriculture—were at the same time devastating to the community of creatures that tried to inhabit the same space as this technological system.

Summer evenings highlighted this. My friends and I could climb to the roof of our barn and see our pastures and the night air above them glowing with the mating rituals of fireflies populating our land; by contrast, the farm fields around us were dark, bleak, and barren. This nightly event was a reminder that our insistence on working with spade and hand rather than by chemical mattered a great deal to the other creatures—insects, birds, and small mammals—who shared the land with us and whose interconnected lives led to a healthy ecology on our small farm.

This darkness was also a reminder of how much this landscape had changed since its caretakers, the Potawatomi, had been removed. With the Potawatomi and other indigenous tribes largely displaced from their ancestral lands,

Euro-American settlers, themselves often displaced by economic processes, were free to turn the landscape into the acres of corn and soybean so quintessential to the modern Midwest. Settlers cleared the land for farms and harvested timber for building, fuelwood, and railroad ties. Of the roughly 20 million acres of old-growth forest that once covered the state of Indiana, about two thousand acres remain.

In her marvelous book *As We Have Always Done*, Leanne Betasamosake Simpson writes about Nishnaabeg internationalism. Anishinaabe, or Nishnaabeg, refers to the culturally related indigenous groups that inhabited the Great Lakes region, including Odawa, Ojibwe, and Potawatomi. To my surprise and delight, she describes internationalism not only as how the Ojibwe relate to Canada and surrounding First Nations but also as how they relate to other species. This is grounded in a traditional story of learning good relations with the deer tribe after a period of overhunting. Seeing different species as nations—deer nation, maple nation—with whom the Anishinaabe are in relationship transforms the landscape into one thrumming with possibility or danger. This is a different sort of international relations. As Simpson says, "Our shared diplomacy has created a relationship that enables our two nations to coexist among many other nations in a single region. From within Nishnaabeg thought, our political relationship with the deer nation isn't fundamentally different from our political relationship with the Kanien'kehá:ka [commonly known as the Mohawk nation]."[11]

Settler colonialism is largely the opposite of this stance. When an empire has learned to see the world as full of resources to be extracted rather than as populated by many nations—people nations, plant nations, and animal nations— to be in relationship with, it becomes easy to assert superiority over any nation. The darkness I saw in the adjoining farm fields in Indiana manifested the lack of political relationship between the white settlers and the firefly nation, the oak and hickory nations, and the Potawatomi nation.

Indigenous removal leads to ecocide. Contemporary indigenous groups vocalize this in their advocacy for themselves and for the ecosystems they are in relation with. For instance, the Baiga, who inhabit an area of jungle in India, declare, "The jungle is only here because of us."[12] Similarly, a statement by indigenous peoples from the Amazon articulates their understanding of the deep interrelationship:

> We have used and cared for the resources of that biosphere with a great deal of respect, because it is our home, and because we know that our survival and that of our future generations depends on it. Our accumulated knowledge about the ecology of our home, our models for living with the peculiarities of the Amazon Biosphere, our reverence and respect for the tropical forest and its inhabitants, both plant and animal, are the keys to guaranteeing the future of the Amazon Basin, not only for our people, but also for all humanity.[13]

Apocalypse means unveiling. But largely, it is not the people experiencing apocalypse who need the truth to be unveiled. It is the settler and their descendants who need the unveiling, who need to see things as they are. I think of the Potawatomi

chiefs Awbanawben and Metea saying to settlers, "You trampled our soil and drove it away," and "The plowshare is driven
through our tents." This is settler land lust. This is colonial
ecology. This is a landscape flayed, layer by layer, as settlers cry,
echoing Herod, "Go on, go on."

The story does not end with displacement and genocide.
Only telling part of this story would perpetuate the all-too-
common idea that all of the natives are gone, reduced to an
unfortunate chapter of world history. Anishinaabe scholar
Lawrence Gross reminds us, "Native Americans have seen the
end of their respective worlds . . . Just as importantly, though,
Indians survived the apocalypse."[14]

Once again, story acts as "imaginative counterpower." In the
Great Lakes, a newer story has begun circulating about Paul
Bunyan, the lumberjack hero of settler colonialism. The Ojibwe
tell us that one of their own legendary heroes, Nanabozho,
fought Paul Bunyan in an epic battle. The stories vary. One
version says that they battled for days and Nanabozho finally
defeated Bunyan and kicked him out of the woods forever. In
another telling, Nanabozho beats Bunyan to death with a fish.

So, too, will the descendants of settler colonists need to
reimagine old stories. New stories don't bring back the many
forests cleared by settlers and their folk hero Paul Bunyan. And
they don't necessarily result in the Potawatomi and so many
others regaining their homelands and indigenous ecologies.
But it strikes me that the root of the problem is in relationships, as Leanne Betasamosake Simpson so acutely perceives.
European settlers need to tell stories not of domination but of
interspecies internationalism, of mutualism and mutual aid.
Perhaps, in the future, children of settlers will walk through

Potawatomi-tended forest ecosystems and tell stories of the blighted days when the trees were gone and the soil was silent and the land was dark, without fireflies. Perhaps they will say that Paul Bunyan laid down his ax and helped Nanabozho nurture the woods of the Great Lakes back to life, so that the beaver and the otter and the deer nations had a homeland again. But that day is far off, and there is much work to be done in the meantime. That work starts with restoring relationships with land and peoples and telling new and different stories, but must end with the rematriation of indigenous homelands back to indigenous nations.

Autumn. I now live in Ventura County, California. Here, where temperatures are mild and sun is plentiful, acres of vegetables and fruit, rather than corn and soy, fill the fields. But still, this is indigenous land, and the loss of indigenous governance to caretake this place has still meant changes in the landscape ecology.

The landscape is much different than that of northeastern Indiana but no less flayed to the bone by settler agricultural and industrial development. Here, at the Pacific edge of colonized lands, there was nowhere farther to push indigenous people. So instead of treaties and promises of land to the west there was tremendous violence, and there was incorporation of indigenous people into the racial strata of white supremacy in the United States.

I am not a farmer anymore. But I keep a garden, and I pay attention to the large fields throughout the county. Agricultural issues are perhaps more complex here on the temperate coast. I think a lot about those Indiana fields, even as I walk

the chaparral hillsides of Ventura or drive past the agricultural
fields on the Oxnard plain. And I lament my lack of answers
for the myriad excoriations of settler colonialism. As Wendell
Berry has noted, there are no large-scale solutions to large-
scale problems. But perhaps we can work toward local and
provisional responses.

I step out of my car with a bucket in hand. It's October, but
still sunny and warm, so I grab my brimmed hat for sun protection. I greet various friends who have gathered in a circle,
and introduce myself to some new faces. Our little assembly
was organized by some Chumash friends. We are here to do
what their ancestors have done this time of year for thousands
of years. We have come to gather. As we spread out under the
trees, I see the ground littered with pointed brown cylinders.
Acorns. I grab a handful, feeling the hardness of the seeds
against my fingers. Into the bucket they go, with a series of
satisfying *clunk*s.

Two main varieties of oak grow here in Ventura County.
Coast live oaks, with their evergreen leaves and curving
branches, dot the hills and valleys. Their roughly oval leaves
often have teeth along the edges. Valley oaks dominate inland.
They tend to grow taller than live oaks, and I think of their
form as a bit more classically knobbed. Oaks are the most
arthritic of the trees, with their bent and gouty limbs, and
valley oaks are especially so.

After an hour of collecting coast live oak acorns, we decided
to go to a different area. Here in the Ojai Valley, we stop at
another park, bare except for two large valley oaks extending their massive shade across the grasses. Excitedly, someone

stoops down and picks up an acorn twice the size of the ones we were finding earlier. "Jackpot!" As I look through the tall grass, I see that hundreds of acorns bigger than my thumb lie all over the ground. Under these two valley oaks, we gather twice as much as we had at the last area.

I return to this acorn-gathering day when I think about how to live as a settler in this Chumash land in Southern California. A day of gathering acorns doesn't undo five hundred years of colonization of the many nations of this continent. It doesn't erase the legacy of displacement and genocide perpetuated by the United States. But being in relationship with Chumash people is a place to start. And paying attention to the gift of the oaks might make more settlers less likely to cut down these nourishing beings.

Across North America, indigenous people continue to resist settler colonialism. Tribes assert their sovereignty by resisting efforts to extract resources or use their lands in unwanted ways. Nick Estes's book *Our History Is the Future* outlines the history of the Standing Rock Sioux and their allies' resistance to the Keystone XL pipeline.[15] In Arizona, Apache Stronghold is a coalition of Apache tribes along with other supporters resisting the mining of a sacred site, Oak Flat, by Resolution Copper.[16]

People living in North America support indigenous people in a variety of ways. In addition to helping resist specific assaults on tribal sovereignty by government or corporate bodies, there are often opportunities to support local or regional indigenous groups. In the Bay Area of California, local tribal groups have a voluntary land tax that people and corporations can offer. The Ramaytush Ohlone of the San Francisco peninsula have a voluntary land tax called Yunakin that people can donate to.[17] On the other side of the bay, the Sogorea Te' offer the Shummi land tax.[18]

On the East Coast, my friends at Silver Run Forest Farm of Virginia donate money as well as plants and trees to indigenous organizations. They explain it this way: "We give away an abundance of plants and we redistribute 10% of what we gain from purchases and donations to people and projects that heal culture, nurture land, and resist white supremacy and colonization, led by those most violently targeted by these oppressive forces and who are leading the beautiful resistance. An advisory council of trusted friends annually helps us discern where this tithe will go."[19] Where settler colonialism has disrupted indigenously cultivated ecosystems, Silver Run Forest Farm cultivates and donates native plants and trees that help to restore lands devastated by settler agriculture.

These are just a few examples of how settlers can act in solidarity with indigenous people reasserting their sovereignty in the lands of North America.

Apocalypse makes imagination a battleground. Colonization has physical and lasting effects, but it starts with the ability to imagine that indigenous people and their ecologies are less important than settler ecologies.

So I think we must first be able to imagine an end to settler colonialism in order to change it. Just as the displacement of indigenous people took sustained effort and attention by those who would benefit from it, so finding a future that upholds the sovereignty of indigenous people and species requires enough people willing to imagine it. That imagination must be formed, I think, in relationships. And what better way to tend to the seeds of imagination than by conversing together as we gather acorns?

AN ANCESTOR, A CABIN, AND A LEGACY

Captain Ware,

I write to you by your honorific not because I put stock in titles but because I don't know what else to call you. It feels wooden, unfamiliar, and distant, but it is the word I have. Many cultures have specific names for their familial relations—an expanded and specific vocabulary of kinship lines—but all I have is a series of *great*-s in front of *grandfather*. I wish I had a more specific word to describe our relationship: you who fathered my grandmother's grandfather: you who settled the Hill Country of central Texas in the 1800s, after helping Euro-American settlers fight against Mexico for the land; you who brought with you six enslaved people. It's now nearly two hundred years later, and I'm grappling with your legacy.

I'm sitting at my grandparents' house in Texas. It's December, but the Texas winter is mild. I look out the window. High gray clouds sit atop the expansive sky. I recall visiting this place as a child and hearing my great-grandmother talk about Captain William Ware, who was one of the first European settlers of this place. She would pack the whole family into the car and drive us a few miles out of town, pulling off to the side of the road. There, from the fence, you could peer between some trees and see the skeleton of a leaning old house in the distance.

"That's the Ware cabin," she said proudly.

I wasn't impressed. Somehow seeing the small, weathered structure deflated the grand, mythic vision in my head.

Over the years, my great-grandmother herself became like your cabin. Her body sagged. She leaned more and more. Her skin became fragile; it tore easily. A hip broke. But she still told stories about the history of family in the area. She died at the age of ninety-one. She is, like you, an ancestor.

I'm older now, and I have more respect for the skills and abilities it took for you to move to a new place, to build a cabin with your hands, and without machines. For you to scratch out life in the semiarid hills of central Texas. Yet I also know that you didn't do it alone. You had enslaved people work for you. Your house was built, most likely, by their labor.

We are not so different. You moved quite a bit in your life. What were you looking for? Was it because of a restlessness of spirit? Or merely a contrariness of nature, an inability to maintain good relations with neighbors?

I am a child of your decisions, a child of colonialism. I grew up in the house you helped to create, this house called the United States of America. This cabin was built by the labor of enslaved black people on land belonging to indigenous people. And as much as I despair over the origins of this house, still, it sheltered me. And I have nowhere else to live.

I was reminded of the predicament recently, in a conversation with a California Chumash man. Matthew Vestuto is bringing back Mitsqanaqan, the Ventureño Chumash language. The language is very old—Chumash people are known to inhabit the coast of California for at least ten thousand years and probably closer to sixteen thousand years. The language is officially extinct—the last known speaker of a Chumashan language died in 1965. But Matthew is relearning the language. In the early twentieth century, a man named John Harrington, who studied ethnolinguistics, took vast notes on Chumash culture and language. From these notes, Matthew has taught himself the language.

One day Matt and I walked along the shoreline in Santa Barbara, talking about a recent conference we had both attended that was centered on the theme of indigenous justice. Eucalyptus trees in the distance evoked the memory of conversations with Brooke, an Aboriginal woman from the land known as Australia, who also attended the conference. She had strikingly described the many eucalyptus trees she saw in California as her fellow countrymen. Two pieces of information, one from each side of the Pacific Ocean, make this significant. First, as she told us, indigenous Australians consider eucalyptus, or gum trees, sacred. Second, many Californians consider eucalyptus trees horribly invasive, and hence scorn them.

The word *eucalyptus* comes from Greek and means "well-covered," referring to the flowers, covered with a sheath that protects them but drops off during flowering to reveal the sexual organs. The *Eucalyptus* genus contains more than seven hundred species, but overwhelmingly, the blue gum (*Eucalyptus globulus*) dominates the California landscape. The tree grows to immense heights, reaching more than 300 feet in

ideal conditions and regularly attaining 150 feet. Its bark
sheds as it grows, creating a natural mulch filled with oils that
make it difficult for fungi to break down the lignin. This combination of bark shedding and flammable oils creates ideal fire
conditions and represents one of the competitive strategies of
the species. This species is an arsonist. It resprouts easily from
the root base after a fire and thus can withstand the flames it
perpetuates. Blue gums stand tall and muscular, with limbs
smooth and gray after shedding bark, while drooping bluish-
green leaves secrete oils smelling of menthol. The tree is a
beauty for multiple senses.

As US settlers arrived in California in the nineteenth century, horticulturalists soon began looking for trees that could
grow in the relatively treeless, semiarid chaparral landscape of
Southern California. Among the trees tested, eucalyptus stood
out. It could withstand the long, hot, dry season but with regular and adequate water could grow rapidly. This combination
of traits made it ideal to plant as a windbreak for orchards and
farms, and at the time it was thought to be a good timber tree.
Soon, though, people realized that the wood warps and twists,
making it poor lumber for building.

Now many consider blue gums invasive. The trees grow easily
in many of the climates of California. "Invasive" is a contested
concept in ecology. It refers to species that are introduced—
intentionally or unintentionally—rather than native and that
cause harm to other native species.

By this rubric, *Eucalyptus globulus* seems to fit the term. The
trees hoard water and mineral resources. Allelopathic chemicals secreted by the roots prevent many other species from
growing in proximity. The plant's fire-promoting features

serve to burn away competition. It outcompetes other plants for water and greedily sucks groundwater to feed its thirsty fibers. On the other hand, gum trees create interspecies relationships in the California context. One study showed that eucalyptus stands have the same species richness as the native forest or chaparral: that is, they are host to a variety of distinct species, only the particular species associated with eucalyptus differ from those of other trees. Monarch butterflies rest by the thousands in eucalyptus groves along the coast.

It's nearing winter solstice, and though the day is still young, the sun creeps close to the horizon. My friend Elaine and I ride our bikes along the shores of Lake Casitas, sharing recent events in our lives. Our route takes us to a short but steep hill, and after a few minutes of hard pedaling, we reach the top. We pull to the side of the pavement, dismount, and pop the kickstands on our bikes. We stand on a small hill jutting toward the southeast overlooking the lake. Twenty paces take us near enough to a few eucalyptus trees to see the upper branches. Squinting upward in the dwindling light, we see a bald eagle perched on a branch, just outside its massive nest. Bald eagles were once widespread throughout the state, but their population declined dramatically due to development and the intensive use of the pesticide DDT in the mid-twentieth century. Though pesticides target invertebrate insects and were sprayed on the ground, they inevitably worked their way up the trophic levels of the food chain. The pesticide caused the eggshells of bald eagles and many other birds to thin, leading to low birth rates. By the 1970s, the eagles were listed as endangered. But since DDT was banned, the bald eagle has returned to Southern California. This mating pair at Lake Casitas has already bred chicks for over five years.

We look up at the bald eagle for a few minutes. I don't know enough to determine whether this is the male or female. Whoever it is, it seems to enjoy its perch high on the blue gum.

Back on the Santa Barbara coastline, Matt and I watch coots in a wetland at the edge of the ocean. These black birds walk with awkward bodies, legs not quite long enough to be elegant like flamingos but a bit too long for their rounded bodies connected to a white squat beak. We continue to talk about the eucalyptus. I mention that I don't think *invasive* is a good term for plants, because people are the ones who are invasive.

"These trees did not choose to be here," I say, recalling Brooke's affection for them. "They are just being themselves, living their lives as displaced countrymen of indigenous Australians. They are refugees."

"Kind of a good metaphor for white people," Matt responds.

I nod my head in agreement. A coot in the wetland bobs its head downward, and moments later it comes up with seaweed hanging from its beak.

I've thought a lot about that conversation since then. Matthew and I both know that while many of us have descended from displaced or refugee Europeans, we live not as refugees but as occupiers. On the one hand, it is true that settlers— mostly of white European descent—have, like the blue gum, hoarded resources. We have acted allelopathically, through practices like indigenous displacement in the nineteenth century, and through ghettoization of black and brown folks in the twentieth century, to prevent nonwhite folks from living in the same places. Onondaga elder Oren Lyons says about white settlers, "Every time we [indigenous people] talk about the nonhuman world we always talk about relatives, whereas you always talk about resources." This is a damning observation of the way white settlers have interacted with the landscape of North America and its inhabitants.

Everyone is born into a story, Captain Ware. You and I were born into a long narrative involving the creation of white supremacy, African slavery, and indigenous displacement. When our ancestors, the Wares, arrived in the Virginia colony, this threefold story was already beginning. Western Europe was in transition; the Mediterranean states of Spain, Portugal, Algiers, Naples, and Venice were losing their imperial power, while France, the Netherlands, and England had begun to expand colonial appetites. In 1606, London investors created the Virginia Company. One historian, Wesley Frank Craven, notes that this company was "primarily a business organization with large sums of capital invested by adventurers whose chief interest lay in the returns expected from their investment."[1]

Many of the first colonists were not the benefactors of this enterprise, however. In its propaganda the company explained that it was performing a public service by removing the "swarmes of idle persons" in England and taking them to the New World. Many English poor were forced into indentured servitude and sent to work in the colony. But the colonists struggled to transplant their way of life to Virginia. Starvation was common, and life was short. Of a shipment of 165 children sent to the colony, after five years only 12 remained.

The Virginia Company began with malicious intent toward Native Americans. Instructions to Thomas Gates, governor of the colony, in 1608 called for forced conversion of indigenous people of the area to Anglicanism and to the governance of the administration. The company also called for kidnapping Powhatan children in order to teach them English ways, a genocidal tactic that would later be expanded and refined in the boarding schools of Canada and the United States. By 1610, relations with the Powhatan had soured such that a war commenced. The early decades of Virginia saw intermittent warfare between the colonists and the indigenous people whose lands they occupied. Francis Bacon justified the colonization of indigenous lands shortly after a Powhatan attack on the Virginia colony in 1622: "Wild and savage people are like beasts and birds, which are ferae naturae, the property of which passeth with the possession, and goeth to the occupant."[2] Thus began the multicentury affair of colonizing indigenous lands for the express purpose of gaining resources.

The seventeenth-century colony was instrumental in laying the groundwork for slavery. In 1619, the first shipment of Africans, enslaved in Angola, was brought to Point Comfort. There they were sold into indentured servitude. Throughout the century, kidnapped Africans were brought to the colonies and forced, alongside others, to work in the tobacco fields. But after Bacon's Rebellion in 1677, the government and wealthy planters began to shift in their approach to workers. European and Native American servants were allowed to work off their indenture, but Africans had to serve for life. This was codified by legislation in 1682. Twenty-seven years later, "An Act concerning Servants and Slaves" defined enslaved Africans as property.

This is our story, Captain Ware. The ideology of white
supremacy and the institution of African slavery did not have
to be created; the constant genocidal aggression toward indigenous Americans did not have to happen. Men made these
choices. And, as best I can tell, most of our ancestors chose to
perpetuate these forces.

Records of court cases and land patents show that Peter
Ware III was in Virginia by 1647. There are smatterings of
Wares noted in the pages of early official papers, and these
indicate that the Wares were associated with the wealthier
landowning classes. I don't know what Peter Ware thought
about the wars with Native Americans, about importing
European and African indentured servants. He did not, like
some Europeans, choose to live with the indigenous nations
nearby. He did not flee to the maroon communities like some
English, Irish, and African people who left the colonial towns
to establish more egalitarian spaces. Like you, Captain Ware,
and me, he seemed to benefit from the power relations set in
place by the Crown and had no moral or economic incentive
to try to change those relations.

Can you be a good settler? I don't know the answer to this
question. My friend Randy thinks it is possible. I first met
Randy, who is from the United Keetoowah band of Chero-
kees, when I lived in Oregon. He would admit that he is a
settler on the land where he lived in western Oregon, which
is ancestral Kalapuya territory. But he points to the history of
good relations between native people of the Pacific Northwest and trappers and traders from Europe who settled the
area before the United States acquired the Oregon Country.
Randy and his wife, Edith, modeled appropriate settler ethics

when they visited tribal leadership in the area and asked how they could honor the Kalapuya.

Similarly, Potawatomi biologist Robin Wall Kimmerer points to the common plantain, a plant that was unintentionally brought over by colonists but that has developed mutualistic relationships throughout the country. She suggests that, as with the plantain, it is possible for settlers to naturalize by creating mutualistic relationships with the native species of this land.[3] I am against easy answers, though these suggestions are not necessarily easy.

Plants interact largely through their roots. But what if the roots of whiteness are allelopathic—that is, toxic? *Rootlessness* is a word commonly used to describe the transience and general lack of historic and place-based knowledge associated with whiteness. I would argue that the problem is not that we don't have roots but, rather, that those roots are disconnected from other people, from place, from history. Just as we know that the roots of almost all plants depend on mutualistic relationships with mycorrhiza, those fungi that live in reciprocal interdependence with plants, rooted cultures live entangled with the other species of their places that sustain them in a nurturing and reciprocal way. The sins of my ancestors were not their decisions to uproot themselves—my understanding is that most of my ancestors left Europe because of economic pressures. No, the problem was not their uprooting but their failure to establish mutualistic relationships when transplanted. And that refusal to recognize the humanity of kidnapped Africans, or to recognize the land tenure of indigenous Americans, impacts my own life. I think of the indigenous wisdom, attributed to the Haudenosaunee Confederacy, of considering how one's actions will impact the seventh generation. Similarly, the Jewish formula, found in the Torah, says that the sins of the parents will reverberate to the third and fourth generations. There is wide indigenous acknowledgment that we inherit the deeds of our forebears.

I visited the Ware cabin again in my adulthood, and it still stands, despite the cracking logs and sagging joints. In the latter half of the twentieth century, a metal roof was built over the weathered building to protect it. The legacy of white settlement persists, buttressed by a protective structure.

What does it take to be a good ancestor? To be good kin after one's life is over starts with being good kin in life. And this, for white settlers, means dismantling the house that white supremacy built. It means making reparations to the descendants of enslaved Africans who built the economy of this nation with their sweat and blood. It requires restoring broken treaties and compensating Native Americans for land and cultural theft. In short, it requires what we might call practicing good internationalism, by honoring all the tribes and nations with whom we are in relation. We must care for bird nations because they keep the world alive with song. And we honor our treaties with Native American nations because they have for so long kept the continent teeming with life, because they can teach us how to be in right relationship with the other nations here, and because it is the right thing to do. What might it mean to raise up the next generations of all the plant, animal, and people nations of this continent just as the eucalyptus at Lake Casitas holds aloft the nest of the bald eagles?

Most white settlers cannot imagine the tables of power being turned. To think of Native Americans having the power to decide whether and, if so, how the children of European settlers are to continue to live in North America is unbearable because we know deeply the extent to which our ancestors in such a short time created a legacy of plunder and genocide. The difficult work is to partner with other settler folk in solidarity with indigenous nations (if and when invited) for the decolonization of tribal lands. Once that happens, the challenging conversation about what to do with us settler children can happen. Maybe we will have a relationship with Native Americans and land that makes it possible for us and our children to continue living in this place. But maybe not. Knowledge of the outcome should not impact whether we support indigenous movements for liberation and sovereignty.

The sins of the ancestors mean that I, and many folks like me, are uprooted. White Americans inhabit an in between place, with no country to call home. We must be willing to navigate this in-betweenness not because there is an end place where we might belong but because there is a possibility of being transformed. We cannot claim a place, and perhaps cannot even be claimed by it. But we can love it. And that sets the stage so that our descendants can have right relationship with the land and its indigenous inhabitants. Perhaps just as decisions of our ancestors carry on into the future and impact the lives of the generations afterward, including our own, our decisions to love the land and its people might at once heal backward and forward.

And that is my hope, for myself and, Captain Ware, for you.

FINDING OUR WAY HOME

I flopped my depleted body on the ground, disregarding the dirt and barely missing a low alpine cactus on the edge of the trail. Tipping a dry canteen to my mouth, my tongue searched for residual moisture around the rim. None. I had drained it hours ago. The moon rose red in the dark night, casting little light but reminding me just how long I had been hiking. I thought back to the earlier events of the day—the morning wake in a desert canyon, the serendipitous midday dip in a refreshing waterfall, and now a long upward hike for hours beginning in the hot sun turned now into a stumbling night hike with desiccated lips, tired thighs, and no water. I surveyed the rest of the group. Like me, all were arrayed in various positions of exhaustion on the ground: one bent over, dry heaving, while another was already asleep. We were on day three without food, and now six hours and eight miles from our last water source.

Looking up at the night sky, I reflected on why I was here, punishing my body in the mountains and canyons of the desert Southwest. It was because of Thomas Merton, the late, intrepid Trappist monk. A few months ago, a friend relayed a quote from Merton's last lecture, just hours before he died in Thailand. Speaking to a conference crowd in Bangkok, he quoted Tibetan abbot Trungpa Rimpoche, whose advice to a younger monk in the face of advancing Chinese army was "From now on, brother, everybody stands on his own feet." Merton went on to apply this sentiment to the inner transformation required of the monastic life:

> We can no longer rely on being supported by structures that may be destroyed at any moment by a political power or a political force. You cannot rely on structures. The time for relying on structures has disappeared. They are good and they should help us, and we should do the best we can with them But they may be taken away, and if everything is taken away, what do you do next?[1]

When I heard this word from Merton, I was intrigued and inspired. He was talking about the monastery and monastic orders, but by the same token, the global systems that underlie everyday life are similarly fragile. Recent events in my life had manifested this. The economic collapse of financial markets in 2008 revealed the fragility of the market economy; the 2012 drought in the Midwest broadcast the brittleness of the food system I had experienced while farming; the devastating hurricane that hit Houston in 2017 exposed the weakness of urban life in the face of climate change. If Merton took standing on one's own two feet to be a metaphor for the spiritual life, my hypothesis was that this two-footed standing must be at the same time physical. Furthermore, if I was to truly

critique contemporary life, I had better strive for independence from it.

Faced with Merton's words, I decided to enroll in an out-
door survival course, to practice nonreliance on empire, and to
learn, as Merton suggested, to stand on my own two feet. So
here I was under the dark desert sky, thirsty, exhausted, and
lying on a pile of dried-out cow manure. I silently cursed at
Merton while my groupmates around me rested, oblivious to
my musings.

Over the course of the next two weeks, I joined a group of
other students to learn about how to navigate desert canyons
and mountains, about ways to find water, about the basics of
trapping small game, and about the plant-based food sources
available in the area. The calls of birds became familiar. Mos-
quitoes were just a mild nuisance. Further, I acquired skill in
building simple shelters and began to feel comfortable sleeping under the night sky without a tent or sleeping bag. I wel-
comed the dark of night rather than dreading the oblique
shadows and unknown noises. I learned to "see with my feet,"
walking carefully but confidently in the dark.

In short, what was once wilderness to me became, for two
weeks, home. This should have been no surprise. The desert is
littered with archaeological remains—pottery shards, knapped
flint rock, and petroglyphs can be found in almost every cave
and rocky overhang. These sandstone canyons and lush desert
springs mark the contours of home for the Zuni, Hopi, and
Diné. Their livelihood seems to have consisted mostly of the
same pursuits as mine; the water sources I sought out were the
same places where I saw evidence of these ancestral people,

because they needed water too. Moreover, petroglyphs etched into the rock showed their appreciation for art, and pottery and flint in small caves made evident their need for food and shelter.

I learned a lot about my body during that short period in the austere desert. As the excess of modern life is stripped away, it is much easier to hear the true desires felt by the architecture of bone, sinew, organ, and flesh. Hunger, though ever present, was not crippling. Water full of particulates still tasted sweet in the hot sun. Wild buffalo berries, though not a significant calorie source, still flooded my belly with the feeling of nourishment. Values transformed over the days. A handful of nuts mattered much more than a headlamp. Mosquito repellant was not worth the weight and subsequent energy required to carry it. What mattered most was what would most immediately allow my body to sustain itself.

In 1972, biologists Humberto Maturana and Francisco Varela introduced the term *autopoiesis*.[2] The word, constructed from Greek, puts together "self" and "creation," to give language to the metabolic magic that all living organisms constantly conjure. By this definition, life is the organization of molecules into a bounded system that maintains itself against entropy or decay. Living means there is a border between the atoms of "me" and "not me." Staying alive requires constant vigilance at that edge: keep the decay outside; sustain the order of the inside. Autopoiesis gives name to this self-creation that makes an organism. As Andreas Weber puts it, "Life makes a lump of matter deeply invested in preserving its particular form and its own freedom to act."[3] Atoms organized around a "me" and aware of the "not me" create life. This identity, shared by the smallest organism to the largest, exists by the primal ethos "Persist! Keep living!"

But the nature of entropy—that movement of energy from order to disorder, from lumpiness to evenness—means that things fall apart. Constantly. Free radical molecules disrupt the genes of a bacterial cell. Heat loss threatens the thermal requirements for the mouse. Desire for continued existence moves the organism to work against decay and entropy by developing ways to produce the energy needed to repair itself, or to seek sources of energy outside itself. Meaning becomes quite clear for the organism. The oak finds that rich soil is good—that is, helping the tree stay alive—and that shade is bad—that is, limiting the tree's ability to fight entropy by channeling energy.

What Maturana and Varela articulate explicitly I found tacitly during my days in the desert. All living beings have an innate desire to keep living, and so do I. We are bound by this impulse and find value in it.

We are matter making meaning.

The distinction between an organism and its surroundings is quite slippery. The "me" and the "not me" can be difficult to define. Water constantly moves into and out of the organism, as does energy. So what is the difference between a molecule of water that is inside a cell wall and the same molecule outside a cell wall? As biologist J. Scott Turner explains, "It is not the boundary itself that makes an organism distinctive, but what that boundary does. In other words, the boundary is not a thing, it is a process, conferring upon the organism a persistence that endures as long as its boundary can adaptively modify the flows of energy and matter through it."[4]

It is not only the nebulous boundaries at the surface of animals and other organisms that show the interconnectedness of life. Organisms often manipulate their environment to expand that process of directing energy and matter flows for their benefit. They extend the "me" of identity outward, organizing external atoms to support their flourishing. This happens in the life of the common earthworm, the singing burrows of the mole cricket, and, finally, the actions of simple human technologies.

A year before he died, the British naturalist Charles Darwin published a lesser-known book about earthworms, *The Formation of Vegetable Mould through the Action of Worms*. In it, he marvels at how such a small creature can have such an impact on the environment. The apparent sinking into the landscape of large rocks, Darwin shows, is actually due to the soil-building actions of earthworms. He estimates that in his area, Kent County, earthworms build soil at a rate of eighteen tons per acre. More recent studies confirm the enormous service that earthworms offer—they churn more than a thousand tons of soil per hectare every year in tropical savannahs.

I remember marveling, like Darwin, at earthworms as a child: the slick wriggle as they escaped my fingers, their ability to slip into the boundary of the soil, the writhing of so many on the surface of the ground after a hard rain.

Earthworm physiology is key to their massive impact on the earth. They have neither an internal skeleton nor the sort of exoskeleton found in many insects. Instead they have what scientists call a hydrostatic skeleton: in other words, the maintenance of internal pressure outward on their outer layer of skin is what enables them to keep their shape. Because of this, earthworms must be constantly vigilant against the desiccating effects of the dry air and soil, which could cause death by dehydration. At the same time, like other animals, they rely on oxygen to survive. These dual needs for air and moisture mean that these squirming creatures have quite a narrow range of environs they can thrive in. It must be aerated but at the same time very damp.

Earthworms accomplish this by action that is familiar to most gardeners and prized by organic farmers. They create burrows in the soil by eating soil and expelling fecal pellets full of aggregated intestinal mucus and soil particles. Passage of dirt through their intestines mixes the particles with beneficial bacteria, and the resultant castings left in tunnels enrich the soil. Their feasting makes soil fertile. In addition, the worms secrete mucus from their skin, which along with the pressure of their bodies through the soil leaves tunnels that are quite stable. They also pull dried leaves and other plant matter into their burrows, storing food for later. Darwin observed earthworms using organic matter to plug the mouth of their tunnels, presumably to inhibit evaporation. These actions are a by-product of their feeding and general movement, but they also create a soil horizon that meets their physical needs: tunnels aerate the soil, while increased organic matter and fecal castings retain more moisture in the soil depths.

J. Scott Turner argues that this process supplies earthworms with an external kidney.[5] Whereas many animals have internal kidneys, an organ that serves to maintain the proper balance of water and salts within the body, the earthworm's modification of its environment makes the rich soil itself an outer kidney. Without the enriched soil, an earthworm could only inhabit a very narrow margin of soil that is both wet enough and oxygenated enough to allow it to live. The earthworm extends its body into the environment in order to expand its dwelling place. Thus, when I harvest the casting-rich soil in my vermiculture compost to add to my garden, in a very real sense I am an organ thief.

Other creatures similarly modify their environment to extend their own bodies. Like many other male crickets, mole crickets chirp by rubbing their tough outer wings together in order to attract a mate. This class of crickets is named after their habit of creating subterranean burrows. But in addition to using the burrows for shelter from prey, male mole crickets also use the burrow entrance as a horn to amplify the sound. The louder they can amplify their fiddle-like vibration, the more likely it is that a female cricket will hear their orchestrations and seek them out for a mate. These insects create a funnel-shaped entrance by widening the mouth of their burrows. This trumpet of dirt amplifies the singing of the cricket. Like a musician with a keen sense of sound, they then emit a short chirp (which females cannot hear) and modify the shape as needed until it is tuned to the frequency of their fiddle and can amplify sound to at least sixty decibels. Once satisfied with the quality of their instrument, they place themselves at the optimal location within the funnel and begin their serenading. Thus, the dirt-trumpet becomes an organ of their body. It enlarges their song of desire.

So, too, we humans extend our bodies.

My earliest memory is of touching fire. I was two or three, and I sat at the dinner table with my parents. My mother lit a candle. I was instantly drawn to the flame, a dancing light, a silent siren song. I had no shipmates, no mast, no cordage to bind me. I stood up in my chair, desperate to touch this flickering beauty. I reached for the brilliant blue edged in orange light. Suddenly, a pain as bright as the flame itself. The rest of the memory is a blur—cries, my mother's fussing, the cold of water on my hand.

Fire seems to be an early memory of the whole of humanity. Across the world, many cultural myths speak of humans gaining fire, usually as a gift from other-than-human beings. For the Greeks, it was Prometheus who stole fire from the gods to give to humanity. Northern Europeans tell of Loki bringing fire to humans. Maui brings fire to the Hawaiian Islands. Many Native American cultures say that Coyote brought fire.

Flame and ember have extended the human body for thousands of years. Heat from fire fractures chemical bonds, allowing the body to access more nutrients more quickly from both vegetables and meat. Cooking foods reduces the energy expended as well, as cooked food is already somewhat broken down and does not require as much chewing prior to swallowing. Flames are thus a sort of external stomach, partially digesting food before it enters the body. One stream of thought suggests that cooking food was largely responsible for the development of the enlarged brain of *Homo sapiens*, due to the increase in nutrients associated with this external digestion.[6]

Fire also creates an external source of heat. All organisms require some parameter of temperature in order to maintain the functions that create that fuzzy boundary between their bodies and the world. Mammals utilize the energy generated by their internal metabolism to fuel their internal temperature. Mitochondria, that small organelle within animal cells, serves as an internal furnace kept alive by the constant addition of food as fuel. But because the temperature of most environments is lower than that of the human body, even the heat from so many mitochondrial furnaces cannot keep the body warm enough.

Humans have found a few ways to protect against heat loss. Clothing acts as a second skin, both to protect from external insults to the body and to provide an extra boundary against thermal loss. Shelter acts as an additional, bigger boundary of the body. A well-built shelter likewise keeps heat within while protecting the inside from wind, rain, cold, and even too much direct heat from the sun. But it was the discovery of fire that drastically changed humans' relationship to cold. Whereas clothing and shelter merely slowed heat loss, fire actually adds heat. Glowing embers were like one's own personal sun, radiating thermal energy so potent it could burn.

So I was excited to learn how to make fire in this desert survival course. Fire would be my extended stomach, my heat, my light. I spent a few days gathering and honing materials. I found a flat sandstone rock and spent the better part of a day slowly boring a depression into it with a hard, sharp piece of granite. This was the top of the apparatus. Next, I spotted a large sagebrush with a thick, straight stem. The woody part of this plant is already quite dry and can burn immediately after harvesting rather than needing days to dry in the sun. From the sage wood I carved a hearth board flat and about a half inch deep. A hole drilled shallowly at the edge of the hearth would be the lower resting point of the spindle. I whittled another piece of sage wood into the spindle, the round piece that would drill into the hearth and create embers. Finally, I created the bow with a piece of willow sapling as long as my forearm, tying twine to each end.

The hearth board lay on the ground, my foot pressed on the edge to steady it. Under the side I placed a large flat piece of bark to catch the embers. I kneeled, placing the spindle into the shallow hole in the hearth. Bowstring wrapped around the spindle. My hands gripped the sandstone sitting atop the spindle, keeping it in place. Slowly, I began to push the bow forward and backward, causing the spindle to turn within the divots of the sandstone on top and the hearth below. Progress was slow as I learned the mechanics: push down on the sandstone too hard and the spindle cannot turn, too light and the spindle jumps out of the hearth and flips out of the bowstring. My muscles were not accustomed to this kind of movement. The spindle fell out multiple times. My arms ached from the back and forth of the bow, the downward pressure on the sandstone top. But soon the spindle was drilling into the hearth. I started to sweat from the effort. Smoke rose from the shallow hole with the lovely smell of burning sage. Black char fell from the hole at the side of the hearth board onto the bark, and as the spinning continued, a pile of smoking charred dust formed. My arms were exhausted, but I continued the steady bowing.

Eventually the dark pile began smoking. I slowly lifted the sandstone, the spindle, the hearth, careful not to disrupt the smoking embers. I lifted the bark and the ember caught in the wind, glowing red. I turned the bark, knocking the ember into a nest of kindling—strips of juniper bark wrapped around each other—and lifted the nest to my face. I blew into the nest, oxygenating the ember that now was smoking more and more, each breath causing a pulse of red to emanate from it. Finally a flame leapt from the nest. Startled, I dropped the ball of fire. On the ground, it continued to burn, and I quickly placed the flaming nest into a prepared collection of twigs and kindling. My arms were tired. My heart pounded. I was elated. I had made fire.

Fire-making. Water-finding. Shelter-building. Food-gathering. Like the earthworm modifying its environment to make it more inhabitable, basic skills allowed me to survive in a place that seemed otherwise dangerous.

What I learned in the desert is that there is no wilderness— there are only people without the cultural knowledge and personal skills to live in certain places. After all, what to me was dry and desolate wilderness was and is home to many indigenous people, and had been so for thousands of years. Indigenous people inhabit numerous places that civilization calls wilderness, from the frozen northern tundra to the barren Sahara to the dense and crawling rain forests.

Wilderness is a concept wrapped up in colonialism. When European empires began to colonize the Americas, they did so under the narrative framework that this "new world" was mostly uninhabited, a vast expanse of land ready for the taking. This, of course, was not true—indigenous civilizations had been inhabiting the Americas for millennia, molding and shaping the land and its ecosystems. Captain

John Smith marveled that he could gallop a horse through the eastern deciduous forest, a possibility only because of the way the forest had been carefully managed with fire to clear the understory.[7] When celebrated naturalist John Muir hiked through the beautiful landscape of California, what he saw as untouched ecosystems were in fact carefully tended by the indigenous people of the land.[8]

Historian William Cronon argues in his essay "The Trouble with Wilderness" that wilderness remained fixed in American mythology as settler ideology. American Indians had to be removed from their ancestral lands in order to maintain the lie of an uninhabited landscape that frontier people could tame. Similarly, national parks were created by removing their original inhabitants in order to perpetuate the dogma of the unpeopled wilderness. He names the predicament of this colonial logic succinctly: "Wilderness embodies a dualistic vision in which the human is entirely outside the natural. If we allow ourselves to believe that nature, to be true, must also be wild, then our very presence in nature represents its fall. The place where we are is the place where nature is not."[9] Herein lies an important concept. Drawing a line too sharply between humans and the other-than-human world allows for violence and extraction rather than the more relational mode of tending.

This dichotomy between nature and civilization is an old story. British archaeologist David Wengrow discusses how the architecture of the Ancient Near East emphasizes the royal program to turn violence into order: palace scenes from Assyrian king Sennacherib's reign depict, in the outer arena, military aggression into distant lands, while inner sanctums show enslaved people constructing the city.[10] Stone friezes highlight in hard relief an imperial politics of external violence legitimized by internal order, applied to both people and nature. Similarly, the earlier Assyrian king Tiglath-Pileser I proclaimed his extraction of trees as a symbol of his dominion over conquered landscapes: "I took cedar, box-tree, Kanish oak from the lands over which I had gained dominion—such trees which none among previous kings, my forefathers, had ever planted—and I planted (them) in the orchards of my land." The ruler's exotic garden became a synecdoche for military supremacy. This early empire used ritual, art, and even gardens to communicate an ecology not of kinship but of chaos and control.

Despite this binary glorifying civilization through the rhetoric of progress, historical evidence shows that people often left empires for more freedom. Anthropologist David Graeber notes that the first documented word for "freedom" was the Sumerian *amargi*, meaning, literally, "return to mother."[11] Old Babylonian codes contain numerous laws concerned with the problem of runaways and how to return them to their work. James C. Scott observes that even the earliest Mesopotamian city-states had walls erected to keep subjects in, a function just as important as keeping enemies out.[12] Similarly, in colonial America, the English settlers reported difficulty in convincing liberated European captives to leave the indigenous villages and way of life they had experienced. Governor Colden of the Province of New York wrote in the early eighteenth century: "No argument, no entreaties, no tears . . . could persuade many of them to leave their Indian friends. On the other hand, Indian children have been carefully educated among the English, clothed and taught, yet there is not one instance that any of these would remain, but returned to their own nations."[13]

In the midst of this ancient dichotomy perpetuated by empires, hill dwellers in the region of Palestine told a different story, passed down into written form in the book of Genesis. For these people, the entire creation is viewed as home. Theologians note that the structure of the creation story manifests this idea. The first three days set up niches—light/dark, sea/sky, and land—that in subsequent days swarm with beings inhabiting them. This lays the groundwork for a theology of inhabitation. This pattern of habitat formation and then indwelling sets the context for the rest of the book. One need not be Jewish or Christian to live into the fundamental premise of this story: the good earth is a place where creatures can find a home that offers what they need to thrive. Likewise, indigenous ecologist Raymond Pierotti reminds us, "what we call nature is conceived by Native peoples as an extension of biological man, therefore a [Native] never feels 'surrounded by nature.'"[14]

Scientists have proposed niche construction as a theory to understand the relationships between individual species and ecosystems (a relationship long known by indigenous wisdom and merely lost to Euro-Americans). Niche construction asserts that species create the environment most suitable for them. For instance, chaparral ecologies set conditions amenable to wildfire, since many of these species benefit from natural fires sweeping across the landscape, bringing nutrients into the soil and eliminating competitor species. Lemon ants in the Amazon use formic acid as an herbicide to remove plants unsuitable for their habitation. Beavers create dams producing larger wetlands, which in turn lead to more riparian trees beavers can utilize for food and habitat.

The earth thrums with aliveness. Soil rises slowly with the steady work of the worm, then erupts suddenly with anthills. Waterways slow and spread outward with the activity of beavers. Gophers incise the earth, leaving tunnels in their wake. Long after the gopher is gone, these arteries will allow water to soak into the ground and will provide habitat for insects and small animals. For these creatures, extending their bodies entangles them in a matrix of a multitude of lives. It is a tangled web, certainly, and not benign. After all, there are spiders in the web of life, as well as snakes, parasites, and a host of creatures whose own lives depend on cutting short the lives of others. But for most creatures the pursuit of life adds richness to the landscape's texture rather than depleting it. Again, Raymond Pierotti instructs on the indigenous ecological knowledge reflecting this entanglement:

> Although the idea of cycles, or circles, of life, is an integral part of Indigenous spiritual beliefs, these are not mystical concepts, but a practical recognition of the fact that all living things are literally connected to one another. As a result of these connections with the nonhuman world, Indigenous peoples do not think of nature as "wilderness," but as home. Natives do not leave their "house" to "go into nature," but instead feel that when they leave their shelter and encounter nonhumans and natural physical features that they are just moving into other parts of their home.[15]

So, too, with humans. The Jewish creation story places humans in this same matrix of niche construction and inhabitation so crucial for thriving. While the phrase "leave no trace" was well intentioned, a better understanding of our relationship to the world would be to "leave good trace." The Chenchu, an indigenous group in India threatened with removal from their homeland, described this relationship beautifully: "Without us, the forest won't survive, and without the forest, we won't survive."[16] Humans and their ecologies are bound together.

Ten days into my survival experience, I spent three days alone at the edge of a small creek winding its way along the base of a white sandstone feature. Despite having successfully made a bow-drill fire multiple times the week prior, now my newly honed skill failed me—I could not start a fire. I made many embers, pressed the spindle into a carefully carved base of sage wood, and drilled rhythmically with a bow made of willow. But multiple attempts to enchant that smoking cinder into a flame with subtle fiber and air were all met with defeat. I cursed the hearth board when it broke, and hurled the spindle across the stream.

The truth is, I need community to stay alive. My two-footed standing in life is bookended by a toddler's crawl and, if I live long enough, a weak-kneed old man's frailty. My very digestion depends on the metabolic activity of the microbiome in my gut. Throughout our lives, we rely on others to care for us. And beyond the human community, we cannot live without other creatures.

How might we survive the many unfolding catastrophes of this age? Not as individuals surviving wilderness but, rather, by communities learning to live again in the contours of landscape and relationship ingrained in the world. It might be possible for humans to find our way home, to reclaim earth as habitat, becoming, as Robin Wall Kimmerer put it, *naturalized*, living "as if this is the land that feeds you, as if these are the streams from which you drink, that build your body and fill your spirit."[17]

Now those cold desert nights are a distant dream. I only occasionally practice fire-making. But I still think often about the lessons of meeting my basic needs. In the cool spring morning, I remember that my coat is a second skin, helping to hold in the heat from the fires of my mitochondria. I leave my house, host to other beings, like the spider whose web drapes the upper corner of the window, and enter into the larger house of my watershed, home to so many other beings. We make this home together, each extending our lives in the ways that suit us. Gopher's house makes tunnels underground that become host to others. Raccoon prowls the backyard at night, occasionally foraging in the same compost heap where earthworms make the soil their kidney. Western gray squirrels make the ground a larder, inadvertently leaving some nuts and acorns to grow into trees, which then become home to other arboreal creatures.

Perhaps if humans, too, found our way home again, we would stop visiting violence upon the external world in our search for internal harmony, replaying that old imperial story. But this is not an individual endeavor. It is not enough to merely stand on our own two feet, but perhaps we can learn, with our human neighbors and the community of creatures in our local bioregion, to stand with our feet, roots, and paws planted in a place we are making together. Naturalized species don't live forever, and neither do survivalists. But the species that have found ways to live among others—those that have entwined their tendrils with other plants, or seduced mycelium into relationship with their roots—do have a home to live and die in. And perhaps that is the answer.

A CATECHISM OF KINSHIP

I stop and squat with my friend Soren at the side of the trail. We are hiking at the base of Mount Hood—called Wy'east by the Multnomah tribe of the Pacific Northwest—an eleven-thousand-foot peak in the Cascades of the Pacific Northwest. The loose, sandy soil left after the snowmelt is the perfect medium to read animal tracks. He points to a cluster of imprints, each with a different depth, orientation, and clarity.

My tracking skills are rudimentary. I sound out the tracks like the letters of a foreign language. I struggle to spot the markings, much less understand what they mean in the context of the other prints in the soil. These look like pawprints—it's a carnivore of some sort. Nearby, hoofprints indicate the presence of deer. In tracking, as in reading, context is everything. As scholars improve their reading of an ancient text by understanding the cultural milieu it was written in, so my amateur knowledge of the animals native to this landscape affects my ability to read the tracks.

Tracks in loose or sandy soil tend to age quickly, even when the imprints sink deep into the earth, like the ones I'm looking at now. That suggests that these grains of sandy soil can be displaced with little effort. A gust of wind or a drop of rain can disturb the indentation. Soil fills it in, and the edges wear down. A good tracker will have knowledge of the climate and soil type; a good tracker can judge the age of a track based on their understanding of how the local weather may interact with the imprint, or how long it will take to blur it to oblivion.

What matters most, though, is not the age of the track but whether it can be followed. Hunters in the Kalahari judge tracks based on whether they are fresh enough to lead to an animal. A track blurred by displacement of particles of dirt or sand is likely old. The fresher a track appears to be, the more likely it is that the hunter can follow it to a live animal.

Trackers are also adept at identifying other signs. They are alert to scent and scat. They consider broken or marked foliage. These signs, or spoor, of various species are learned by trackers and used to understand the intentions of an animal so that they can accurately determine the direction the animal headed.

Excellent trackers seem to have an almost magical relationship to animals and their tracks, born out of deep knowledge and experience. Moose Jackson, a Kluane First Nation hunter, knew animals and their spoor so intimately he could predict by the tracks where the animal would be. Anthropologist Paul Nadasdy spent time with this hunter during field research and observed that he could simply glance at a moose track and know how old it was. Because of his knowledge of the moose and the landscape, Jackson did not even need to follow the tracks, since he knew where the moose would be going.[1]

Tracking is a way of learning that implicates us in the world. We cannot stand apart from it as objective, as science might have us do. Rather, we learn as cocreators and coconstitutors of the world. In tracking, we find that we share this world with others, with whom, if we act in humility, we can live as kin.[2]

An ancient art as old as hunting itself, tracking was perhaps the first instance of hermeneutics. The first human hunters did not have written words but instead interpreted the signs of the landscape, extrapolating the movement and intentions of animals based on the marks they left. For these hunters and their communities, proper exegesis was the difference between hunger and a full belly. To be adept at reading the signs in the soil meant not only greater harmony with the landscape but also the ability to live.

Tracking is thus an exercise in landscape exegesis. Every track is a sign on the manuscript of the world. Tracker Tom Brown Jr. says it this way: "Each track becomes a word and each trail a sentence, a paragraph, or a chapter of an animal's life."[3] Just as the scholar looks at a text in context, the tracker reads the trail: the pen is a paw, the sentence is the trail, the page is the landscape, and the message is the intention of the hunted.

The point of exegesis is to build knowledge of the context of a written text in order to better understand it. Without an understanding of the ancient culture a book or letter was written in, one might read it with modern assumptions about the nature of the world. This is also the case with tracking. The tracker must have a breadth of knowledge of the place—the quality of its soil and how quickly it weathers, the locations of water, the brittleness of various plants in response to creatures rubbing against them, the types of plants and the seasons in which they are most edible for browsing, and the nature of scat from different animals.

The tracks themselves must be correctly interpreted as well. If tracks are like a language, the tracker must learn the syllables and understand the grammar. This requires a steady attention both to how one's own movements affect the landscape and to the unique signs of various creatures. When I take a step, walking slowly across the silty floodplain of the Sandy River that drains into the Columbia, I don't realize it, but I am leaving tracks behind. The earth beneath me responds to the pressure of my foot. To the right, my eyes follow a duck making flight off the river, and as I watch, my weight shifts, leaving deeper ridges on one side of my footprints.

Brown calls the topography of a track a "pressure release." The point of entry, the speed, and the shifting of weight compress the soil or track medium. As the foot is raised from the ground, the combination of entry, velocity, and release creates aspects much like geological features in miniature. The study of these features, or pressure releases, shows that no matter the size of the creature, the same pressures generate the same feature in a track. Thus, trackers can learn from a particular warp in the soil the direction an animal turned its head.

With this knowledge, tracks come alive. Subtle depths in an imprint and minute fault lines denote shifts in the body of an animal, a turning of the head or a changing of course. Small variations in the tracks along a trail indicate increasing thirst or hunger in an animal. A ridge here indicates a wound or limp; a ripple there in the track margin reveals a sidelong glance at some distraction. Just as card players look for tells in the faces of their opponents, pressure releases provide insight into an animal's intention.

This landscape exegesis helps us to understand the world around us. Tracking and nature awareness help us see who we are in the world, and only by knowing our place in the world can we know the gift we have to offer it. Reading the trails of other creatures leads us to reflect on the marks we leave in the world. This reflexivity awakens consciousness. As novices begin to track an animal, it is not long before they perceive that they, too, are leaving a trail of tracks and signs. The track reader is also a track maker.

On a cloudy winter day, I hike with a friend's three-year-old, Daniel. His parents hike ahead of us on the path, but we amble, taking our time. The path along the butte is snowy, and as we tromp through the snow, little Daniel notices the pawprints of dogs alongside the footprints of their human companions. I ask him what his footprint looks like, so he stomps his foot in an undisturbed section of snow by the path. His eyes brighten as he realizes that he too is leaving tracks as he walks. What follows is a joyous jaunt along the trail, with frequent glances backward to see the tracks being created with each step.

As trackers learn to read the signs, a realization happens. They suddenly understand that the earth is a tablet and that all living beings write their story on it each day. An owl leaves small scratches on the tree it grips with its talons. A fox leaves a trail of indentations in the soil and displaces leaves in the grass where it moved its body against them. Deer create paths by their repetitive movements through the forest, wearing out the plants under them and leaving bare, compact dirt. And these stories interact. The young tree scratched by the owl is investigated by a hungry deer; the leaf fibers from that tree are found in deer scat farther down the trail; then, days later, the tracks of the deer stop at the imprints of a mountain lion, and nearby one might spot bones, slowly decomposing and settling into the landscape. The world is full of these stories, and the tracker reads these tales in bent twigs and faint footprints pressed on soil. If each track is the sentence of a story, one learns quickly that the sentences write their protagonists into the undulating plot of the universe.

As they scour the landscape for details, many trackers recount an experience of mental metamorphosis into the animal they are tracking. As Louis Liebenberg describes in *The Art of Tracking*, the hunters of the Kalahari say they feel the sensations of the quarry they are trailing.[4] One hunter explains that as he followed the tracks of a springbok, an antelope species, he began to feel the aesthetics of it. A tickling at his legs and feet told him the springbok was hiding in bushes. A sensation down his nose and around his eyes mimicked the black marks on the antelope's head. As he approached, he felt blood running down his legs, an anticipation of the kill. Just as reading a novel might help modern readers understand the worldview of another person, the hunter, in reading the tracks of the springbok, perceives the world from its point of view. The hunter imaginatively embodies the hunted.

Tracking is a sort of inverted theosis. If theosis—a taking on of godliness—connotes union with the divine, then tracking turns this inside out and unites the hunter with their other-than-human kin. This is not by looking up, as humans have done for so long, with imperial religion's tower and gothic spire, but by turning our gaze to the ground. In tracking, we gain a greater sense of our embodiedness.

As we move across the landscape, chasing tracks and simultaneously making our own, we become more animal. We see in the tangled interface of trails the intricate interplay of life with life. We discover in our own footsteps that our tracks connect to this network of stories. We look in an animal's tracks and see our own search for food, shelter, and companionship reflected back at us. By doing so, we reject the dualism and technologies of civilization that would have us believe we are divorced from the same world inhabited by beasts. In becoming animal, we become more human again.

In the early twentieth century, German biologist Jakob von Uexküll proposed a way of understanding nonhuman life that marked a turn in classical biology. Instead of seeing life as a machine with parts that operate according to code, Uexküll suggested that all life-forms interpret their environment for certain objects of significance.[5] He illustrated this with the life of a tick. The life cycle of a tick depends on the blood of a mammal in order to survive and procreate, therefore a tick's life consists of seeking stimuli that lead it to this nourishing substance. First, photoreceptors help the otherwise blind tick to climb foliage toward the sun, giving it the advantage of height. Next, the odor of butyric acid, present in the blood of mammals, alerts the tick of a passing animal, and it releases its grip from the blade of grass. If the tick successfully lands on the animal, it uses heat-sensitive receptors to find a patch of skin to sink its jaws into and begin the feast.

These three signs—light, butyric acid, and warmth—create the tick's world. Uexküll called this collection of important stimuli the organism's *Umwelt*, or "surroundings." No matter how expansive or small, the umwelt—that collection of meaningful aspects of the organism's world—provides a window into its existence. This theory applies from the smallest known life-forms, such as bacteria, to the largest and most complex. All of life pursues this fundamental behavior of following meaningful stimuli in order to continue to live, and each individual's world, its umwelt, is ordered by this desire for life. For most animals, this includes the perception of water, nourishment, reproduction, and safety.

The lifeworlds of organisms overlap. Any mammal with blood that can nourish a tick becomes part of the meaningful universe of the insect. Some mammals, like chimpanzees, might note the tick as a parasite and pluck it off. On the other hand, for a chicken, the tick itself might announce mealtime. In a more complex animal—for instance, a cat—the array of meaningful stimuli grows exponentially. A wider assemblage of smells becomes important. Senses increase to include sight and sound. Sensorimotor skills develop in relationship to an environment that must be navigated. Scores of animals might be prey. Multiply the number of animals, expand their umwelt, and we arrive at the millions of nodes of interconnections in the web of life.

All tracks decay over time, some more quickly than others. A pawprint in the mud can harden and last for months, while dirt typically erodes in a matter of days. Sounds like the unique *waka-waka* of the red-headed acorn woodpecker make "tracks" in the sky, a medium where signs are even more fleeting. Tracking sounds is its own skill, an exercise in recognizing patterns in the air. Just as a tracker can identify the similarity in form that signals coyote or bobcat, so too can one learn to discern the *caw* of a crow from the *croak* of a raven by the template of pitch, timbre, loudness, and duration that distinguish each. When I pay attention to the unfolding of life around me, I have a deeper understanding of myself as well as the creatures I share this place with. I listen, watch, smell, feel, and sometimes taste the ecosystem I inhabit. I learn the poetry of other beings engaged in being alive, and their aliveness fosters a better sense of my own.

Running on Sulphur Mountain in Southern California, a single-lane dirt road takes me past tar slicks exuding an odor of rotten eggs: this mountain lives up to its name. Live oaks with fire-blackened trunks offer intermittent shade in the summer sun. Occasional breezes whip up dust clouds, and I squint to protect my eyes. The flowering plants of spring have already turned brown and brittle. Despite the muted colors, these chaparral hills thrum with aliveness. This is most evident by the constant birdsong all around. In the oaks, acorn woodpeckers intermittently shout their characteristic *waka-waka*. Dark-eyed juncos emit their high-pitched *chip*s in the underbrush as they forage, while robins, a bit bolder in their foraging in the open, regularly *tut* back and forth as they hop in the meadows and trails searching for insects and seeds.

As I crest a small hill, the oak meadow suddenly hushes. A shadow crosses the trail in front of me. I crane my neck to look up, and see the underside of a red-tailed hawk in the air above. As the hawk glides over the ridge, the chorus starts up again.

All organisms sense their environment. We feel pressure and heat, see, hear, smell, and taste. Our senses help us pursue nourishment, avoid danger, and maintain what the body needs. If we pay careful attention to the birds, they extend our perception of the environment. The hush of the meadow reminded me that day that the song of the birds can tell me a lot about what is happening around me.

Communication across species also occurs through sound patterns. I've never seen a burrowing owl, but I have seen their zygodactyl *k*-shaped tracks in the dirt and sand of Ventura County. These owls often share underground burrows with ground squirrels here in California, or, farther east, with prairie dogs. Owls are typically associated with keen eyesight, which these birds do have. Despite their large eyes, these birds don't just focus on photon-transmitted sight; they also make use of sounds. They live in synergistic relationships with the species with which they share burrows. Though winged, these feathered creatures comfortably stand on the ground for long periods of time and often perch at the entrance to a den to help keep watch for predators. Burrowing owls have been observed to "eavesdrop" on other species. The frantic alarms of ground squirrels or prairie dogs will similarly send the birds into alarm mode and cause them to retreat to their dens.[6] Burrowing owls also listen to the alarms of southern lapwings and show apprehension or hiding behaviors at the sound of a southern lapwing's alarm. Sound mimicry occurs across many bird species, but burrowing owls have learned to imitate the rattle and hiss of rattlesnakes when cornered within their burrows, a sure way to scare off many predators.[7]

We humans also "eavesdrop" on the language of birds. The baseline symphony of the meadow or forest is a general indication that all is well, while the *peek!* alarm of a robin signals potential predators. The sudden silence, like I experienced on my run, can also indicate an imminent threat. These feathered messengers of the air lead author David Abram to connect birds with angels:

> This ancestral sense of the wingeds as messengers, and as guardians of a sort, is preserved for many persons in the conception of angels. (The word "angel" itself comes from the Greek "angelos," meaning "messenger.") The iconography of angels has always shown them with feathered wings ... It is likely that the wondrous qualities ascribed to angels were once associated with the elusive, winged presence of birds themselves.[8]

One example of birds as messengers comes from a formerly enslaved person in the South. Louis, who escaped the plantation and lived in a den in the woods, explained how interspecies allyship helped him: "Can't nobody come along without de birds telling me. Dey pays no min' to a horse or a dog but when dey spies a man dey speaks."[9]

Over time, acts of deep listening can lead to human-bird communications and partnership. The legendary honeyguides of Africa respond to a whistled call from hunters and lead the hunter to a beehive full of honey. The hunter is then expected to share some of the bounty with the feathered guide. Inuit hunters of North America describe calling magic words to ravens, who then lead them to polar bear or caribou.[10] In return the hunter leaves some choice meat for the ravens.

So when we listen to the song of birds, we expand our understanding in real time. Silence, alarm, or birdcalls tell us much about the forest or field we walk in. Through hearing, along with our other senses, we are mapping the world, creating a cosmology, one taste, one smell at a time. We learn through touch that the world does not end at the edge of our fingertips.

All perception is, in fact, a caress, a touch, of sorts. Sensory cells contain hairlike cilia involved in perceiving. Sound waves drum on fluid in your inner ear membrane, converting waves in the air to waves in the snail-shell spiral of your cochlea. Here the fluid waves bend the sensory hairs like kelp floating in an ocean wave, and these sensory cells, when bent, communicate sound to your central nervous system. In your eyes, rod cells have a cilia structure packed with photoreceptors that, when "touched" by photons, send an electrical signal to your brain.[11] Similarly, when molecules from the air dissolve into nasal mucus and contact the cilia of olfactory cells, a neural impulse of smell is sent to your brain. As with smell, food particles in the mouth engage proteins in the ciliary structures of your gustatory cells, allowing you to taste your food. Mechanical pressure bends hairlike projections from sensory cells, allowing your skin to feel. Our senses intimately engage us with the world. As writer Sophie Strand notes, "Life isn't composed of invisible ideal forms that hover beyond the realm of messy, generative embodiment. Life is haptic. Haptic is defined as 'pertaining to and constituted by the sense of touch.' It is derived from the Greek word 'haptikos' which means to come into contact and to fasten."[12] Molecules in our mouth press on the tongue. Light taps our retina. Odors touch our olfactory nerves. Sound waves brush our inner ear. Pressures on our skin stroke corpuscular cell fibers. We are constantly caressed, constantly fastened to the world around us, implicated in the ongoings of life.

We must perceive the world in order to act within it. All organisms chart their environment, a simple form of cognition, so that they can act within it according to their desires. As discussed earlier, the word *umwelt* encompasses all the meaningful perceptions of an organism. The tick smells butyric acid, senses light, feels warmth because it desires to sup on the blood of some unsuspecting mammal. The senses help the tick understand and locate itself within its environment so it can move toward its goal. Understanding is the basis for intention, and perception precedes cognition.

Desire undergirds all of this. As Andreas Weber articulates, "Everything that lives wants more of life."[13] An organism's existence has meaning because it matters to them, so they wish to continue living. Sensing the environment in order to map their situatedness within it enables the organism to act according to this desire. The toadstool longs for shaded rot, which is why its whispering mycelial threads scout the forest floor in search of the perfect mixture of moisture, temperature, and substrate to sporulate in. The acorn woodpecker wants to care for her family, so she surveys the forest for the best larder trees for caching acorns. Whether the oak, content to root toward the tastiest mineral grit and loam, or the tiniest

bacterium, gatekeeping cellular walls to control what nutrient comes in and which metabolic by-product escapes, all life
maps the environment to live longer within it.

Life happens where organisms' desires meet. This leads
inevitably to struggle, trickery, treachery, and sometimes plain
partnership. The antelope wants to survive, while the lion
craves meat. The hyena's and lion's competing hunger leads
to conflict over antelope flesh. Maggots take advantage of the
rotting bodies in the savannah. And roundworms capitalize
on all of these intersecting lifeways by pairing their life cycle
with those of these animals as they infiltrate animal bodies.

Our lives overlap, too, with the lives of other beings in our
ecosystems. At best, our senses give us the ability to act in
solidarity with the other creatures we find kinship with in the
world. When hunters partner with ravens or honeyguides,
they share a cosmology, however brief, with these feathered
ones.

As I learn birdsong, it helps me to imagine it as patterns
in the air. The mountain chickadee's *cheese-bur-ger* tonal song
seems to mean "I am here," a communication to its mate that
all is well. When I hear that pattern, I can infer that the chickadee's safety also suggests my own when I go for a run in the
conifer woods of Lake Tahoe's Rim Trail. Though they may
not intend it, the mountain chickadees share their knowledge
of the environment through vocalizations. If the chickadees
sing, there is not likely a bear or mountain lion nearby, and I
feel more at ease.

Birdsong reminds me that life is full of sense and communication. These winged messengers sing that the world is full
of hawks and threats, yes, but also of desire and partnership,

of mates and offspring. If poetry is a way to produce richness of meaning with words, to be alive is to produce meaning with matter. To listen to birdsong is to eavesdrop on the
poetry of life.

There are not many hunters left in the world who need to
track their prey. But tracking offers a possibility of reading our
relatedness in the dirt, a way to expand our perception of the
world surrounding us. It is the story written in paw and claw
that decenters human supremacy in the saga of life. It is the
script of our overlapping umwelt.

Tracking helps us to better understand the world and our
place in it. As a practice, it widens our vision of the world. We
come to notice the torn grass on a hillside that indicates the
past hunger of a deer. We become aware of our impact on the
world, from the path of our footsteps across a muddy field to
the larger and much more serious imprint of our garbage on
the landscape. Even the weathered pawprints of a dog on a
trail might remind us of both our creatureliness and our corresponding susceptibility to the ravages of climate and time.

You can track anywhere, as animals are everywhere dis-
turbing the landscape, leaving their marks. To track means to
observe the little changes, and cultivating this awareness can
be simple—it only requires intention. To start, find a sit spot.
Make time once a day to go to this spot and just sit. During
sit-spot time, you will begin to notice the creatures that sur-
round you. Document the birds you see. Notice their markings
to identify from a reference book later. Listen to the sounds
at dawn or dusk. Be aware of the alarm calls when a predator,
such as a cat or hawk, approaches and then the silence that

ensues when it is very near. See how a dog hurtling through bushes disturbs the branches with bent or broken twigs.

Next, tune your vision to the details of the landscape itself. Human footsteps across the lawn bend the blades of grass such that, at a certain angle, there is an obvious color differential from the undersides of the upturned leaves. In the city, one can notice a half footprint in the detritus on the edge of the street or in the fallen leaves of autumn. By starting big, with human footprints, your awareness can develop, making it possible to begin noticing smaller things. Find a squirrel on the ground, and study the fresh traces it makes by scampering across the grass or soil as it speeds away. Take advantage of the snow as a way to easily track game through the woods or to imagine the path of people in the concrete jungle of the city. Make use of a sandbox as a medium. Press your shoe into the grains, and watch how wind or rain erodes a footprint.

Most importantly, keep watch. To the one tuned to tracks, life is happening all around. Footprints are being made and weathering away constantly. Trails thread together all around us, weaving a tapestry of stories, and by learning the language of tracks, we may follow the footprints of the persistence of life on the landscape of our lives.

Catechism is a word from the Christian tradition. It derives from a Greek word meaning "oral instruction," which describes the teaching format. The teacher asks a doctrinal question of the student, who responds with the prescribed dogmatic answer. For instance, Martin Luther's Small Catechism gives a series of questions with the answers a believer should give. Despite its name, the full catechism is quite long, but here is a sample:

1. *Do you believe that you are a sinner?*
   Yes, I believe it; I am a sinner.
2. *How do you know this?*
   From the Ten Commandments, which I have not kept.
3. *Are you also sorry for your sins?*
   Yes, I am sorry that I have sinned against God.[14]

When I practice tracking, I often imagine it as a catechism of sorts, but rather than one of religious doctrine, it is a catechism of connection to the broader world we inhabit. I want my instructor to be the watershed I live in. I want to reclaim the practice of catechism, of being queried—not by religious leaders, but by the landscapes of our lives. Marks in the sand, spoor in the bushes, or sounds in the air interrogate the seeker.

Whose paw is this?
   Coyote.
Where is she going?
   To the manzanita.
Who collected these sticks in a large pile?
   Woodrat.
Why did she do this?
   To shelter her young.
Whose song is this?
   White-crowned sparrow.
Why does he sing?
   To enchant his mate. I too am enthralled.

The answers do not enumerate doctrine; rather, they make evident the community of creatures with whom one lives. In reading tracks, or in listening to the poetry of birdsong, I deepen my cosmology. I learn a new catechism, a catechism of kinship:

What do you believe?
That I was born by desire, that I live by the yearning of my cells. That my body is an ecology not of my own making. That I will one day be eaten and will rise again in the sycamore.

Where do you belong?
I belong to this watershed, where the mockingbird sings, where the steelhead trout run when the river flows to the sea, and where the oaks rain gifts of acorns every fall.

Who is your neighbor?
Coyote, woodrat, and white-crowned sparrow are my neighbors. Opossum who scavenges in my backyard is my neighbor.

How do you know these things?
By the photons tapping on my retina, showing me the shape of coyote trotting in the dry stalks of mustard on the hills. By the song of the sparrow washing through my inner ear. By the smell of black sage and artemisia flavonoids touching my olfactory cells on a hot day. By raccoon's print in the dirt of my backyard.

Who are you?
I am a creature, full of desires and disgust and hunger and dreams. I leave traces of my own as I move according to these passions. I am a creature among creatures and live in a place brimming with life. I am surrounded by kin with teeth and chlorophyll and hands and roots and fur and scale, and to all of them I am bound.

HUNGERING BODIES

I am tracking Coyote.

He trots in a straight line—each pawprint direct, conserving energy. He is always looking for food. His scat contains anything or everything. The shiny shells of beetle bodies. Twisted fur from some small mammal. Seeds blackened by a bilious stomach. Scaled skin of lizard or snake. Coyote moves with intention, and scats often. He has an appetite, and he follows his belly.

I jot measurements, draw observations. I am a scribe of Coyote's hunger.

I live on Chumash land in Southern California, and here, as in many places across North America, Coyote is one of the archetypal trickster symbols. As Lewis Hyde shows in his book *Trickster Makes This World*, the trickster figure pursues his appetite, often to his own dismay.[1] One Chumash story about Coyote says that he conjured salmon to jump out of the creek, until the beach was filled with the fish. But Coyote wanted to be able to gorge himself, so he walked across the country to a place with brackish water, so that he could purge his belly and prepare to stuff himself with fish. While Coyote was gone, Blue Jay, watching from a cottonwood the entire time, swooped down and ate and ate. By the time Coyote returned thin and hungry from his purging and his long journey, the beach was empty, and Blue Jay was laughing from the cottonwood, his belly full of salmon.[2]

Desire, Coyote reminds us, shapes the world. To understand a species, simply observe it. Its body and its movement show what it wants. What does the oak tree reach toward? Follow the contours of its fibrous body to light above, and water, mineral, and nutrient below. Want to find a white-tailed deer? Follow its tracks, which will show you what it wants. Water. Fresh herbs. To lie in the tall grass in safety.

We are all children of Coyote, shaped by hunger. Appetite organizes the very structure of our bodies. Animal physiologists observe that every animal body, from the smallest worm to the largest elephant, is fundamentally a tube. We call this tube the digestive tract, or, perhaps more scientifically, the alimentary canal, and we think of it as a series of organs, but in fact it is an opening, a passage, around which every animal is merely a different set of cellular riffs. Merlin Sheldrake observes that while mushrooms and plants put their bodies into food, animals put food into their bodies.[3] The animal body is a hungry cylinder—open, living, and eager to bring the world into it.

Digestion: to break down into nutrients that can be taken up into the body. This definition smacks of violence and prepositions. Break and take, up and down. Somehow in that brutality and directionality magic happens. Something that was outside goes inside and, on the inside, joins the body. Through appetite, through eating, the apple comes to constitute our very bodies.

So grasp the rosy apple. Take a crunchy bite. Do violence to it with your teeth. Taste the sweet fructose. Notice the moist matrix of fruit crushed in your mouth. Let it linger a moment. Roll it on your tongue. Open the gates to your insides. Swallow the mashed bits. Feel your stomach churn. Imagine the chemical warfare of your bile exploding the cellular structure of the apple. Sense the scurry of enzymes cutting carbohydrate chains into pieces. Give the first fruits of the harvest to the bacteria in your gut. They are hungry, and you can afford to let them feast. A taste of the sweetness will agitate them and will wind the metabolic machine of their own enzymes. They will conjure their own alchemical magic onto the mash, and you'll harvest some of the dregs of their work. Sometimes tricksters dupe others into doing the work for them.

Hunger means to want the world to be inside you so that it can become part of you. Yet you are already part of the world. Your inside already belongs to the outside. In a way, digestion breaks down the false boundaries we construct between us and what is not us. The body is a fuzzy boundary. The line between me and not me blurs in the belly, in the billions of bacteria in the gut, in the inhalation and exhalation of air merging and diverging in our lungs. At what point does the Honeycrisp apple in my stomach become part of me? At what juncture does the oxygen count as "body" rather than "air"?

In another story, Chumash villagers of Mitsqanaqan said that Coyote came and ran all over the hill. He couldn't decide what he wanted, so he meandered about, tasting berries, snapping at voles, and scatting everywhere. That's why the water tastes bad: because Coyote shits and shits.[4]

Thus, Coyote embodies the fundamental aspects of being animal in this world. The animal cannot produce its own energy and so must eat the flesh of other creatures that do create their own energy. Coyote stirs up trouble, agitates the existence of other species in order to satisfy his own hunger, the vacuous nature of his digestive tract. In the ultimate boundary crossing, he takes the rabbit's body in, makes the meaty rabbit flesh part of his own. His creativity lies in his hunger. Sometimes that creativity and curiosity give him a feast, and other times just a mouthful of thistles and a belly full of fur.

Coyote stories provide a thick description of the relationship between tricksters and hunger. But there are many other examples. Some of my own ancestors come from Wales, and one story they told along these themes, the legend of Taliesin, provides a study in the relationship between desire, tricksters, and inspiration.

Taliesin, a Welsh bard believed to have lived in the sixth century CE, was renowned for his poetry. The Book of Taliesin, a twelfth-century manuscript, contains Welsh bardic poems attributed to him. He was so renowned that court bards after him took up his persona and claimed the same inspiration that danced across his tongue. The legend of Taliesin, however, survived as much in the countryside as it did in royal halls.

Much of what we know about his story comes from the account written by Elis Gruffydd in the sixteenth century. While the Book of Taliesin contains bardic poetry and thus only references aspects of Taliesin's life, this history of Taliesin purports to tell the entire legend.

In the tale, a powerful woman named Ceridwen sought to create a magical potion that would confer wisdom on the person who tasted three drops of it. That person, according to Ceridwen's plans, would be her own son, who was so ugly he was named both Morfran and Afagddu, meaning, respectively, "Great Crow" and "Utter Darkness." So Ceridwen went across the countryside of Wales collecting herbs, placed them in a cauldron, and set an old blind man to stir the pot for a year. She also conscripted a peasant boy named Gwion Bach to tend the fire.

For an entire year, the blind old man and the young lad went about their work, stirring and stoking, and the herbs congealed into a potent stew, and Ceridwen continued to add herbs and water to the magical brew. Ceridwen knew that after a year, when the recipe was complete, three drops of the elixir would jump from the pot. As the time drew nearer, and the fire was raging and the cauldron bubbling, she stationed her unfortunate son near the pot to catch the elixir of wisdom. She leaned back as she waited, pleased at her work, but fell asleep.

Ceridwen was thus fast asleep when, just as the drops sprang from the pot, Gwion Bach, the fire-stoking peasant boy, pushed Morfran out of the way! The cauldron itself cried out in light of this trickery and shattered, spilling the magical brew. Ceridwen woke from the commotion and looked with poisonous eyes at Gwion Bach. He had a burned tongue and a sudden well of wisdom, but it took neither wisdom nor age for him to know that she had a murderous rage toward him.

Gwion Bach fled. When Ceridwen ran after him, she saw him turn into a hare, bounding like lightning across the fields, so as she pursued, she became a greyhound. Gwion Bach, seeing that she was overtaking him, jumped into the river and became a salmon, while Ceridwen also dove into the water, becoming an otter. And so they went. Salmon to dove, otter to hawk. Finally Gwion Bach came to a barn filled with grain from the harvest, and he became a kernel in the sea of wheat. But Ceridwen, equally clever, became a hen and ate the entire pile of grain, thus devouring Gwion Bach.

But now, with Gwion Bach, the shapeshifter, the thief of wisdom, in her belly, Ceridwen became pregnant. For nine months she carried the child, and in the tenth month, she delivered him. But when she saw the child with his beautiful brow, her murderous rage softened. She could not live with the boy, but she also could not kill him. So she set him in a hide-covered basket and put him out to sea.

Eventually the coracle with the beautiful baby washed into a seine ashore the coast, and there was found by a lord named Gwyddno. On seeing the child, Gwyddno exclaimed, "Taliesin!," meaning "What radiant brow!," and took the child home with him. Taliesin, like Hermes, was a precocious baby, spouting poetry and song even in his coracle. This poetic wisdom led to a bardic vocation, and as long as Taliesin was in Gwyddno's court, wealth came to the lord. There is more to the tale: the lord's boast, a king's jealousy, and a bard's magical words. But those are words for another day.

So the story of Taliesin is a story of boundaries, of theft, of shapeshifting, and, somehow, out of all that, wisdom and poetry. Gwion Bach, in his theft of what was meant for

Morfran, becomes a boundary crosser. In receiving the drops of wisdom, he takes magic that was not meant for him, a peasant boy. Trickery connotes a plan, a premeditation, but the story is not clear on this. Perhaps the year of fire-stoking also sparked a plan in the lad's head. But just as likely, a poor boy with few options saw the sleeping Ceridwen and in the moment took advantage of a once-in-a-lifetime opportunity.

What might it mean to inhabit Coyote, to enliven the landscapes we dwell in? If indeed the world is alive, how does this change how we understand our own contingent, hungry lives? What is the role of humans in the ongoing story of life, which is the tracing of desire, the appetite induced merging of bodies into bodies, at times the hungry crossing and at others the fearful honoring of boundaries?

Foresight was the first gift of the elixir. It does not take a genius to consider the danger presented by a sorceress from whom you stole a year's worth and a beloved son's gift, but then Gwion Bach did not seem to think about this before he tasted the potion. Trickster reads the room and knows when to cut and run. But the real wisdom came, as is clear in multiple poems from the Book of Taliesin, from the shapeshifting pursuit. The bard and those who came after him appear to locate Taliesin's wisdom in his experience of being other than human. One poem, "Angar Kyfundawd," expands the shapeshifting:

> I was a blue salmon,
> I was a dog, I was a stag,
> I was a roebuck on the mountain,
> I was a block, I was a spade,

I was an axe in hand,
I was an augur held in tongs
for a year and a half.
I was a speckled white cockerel
covering the hens in Eidyn
I was a stallion at stud
I was a fiery bull.
I was a stook in the mills,
the ground meal of farmers
I was a grain . . .
It grew on a hill.
I'm reaped, I'm planted
I'm dispatched to the kiln
I'm loosed from the hand
in order to be roasted.
A hen got hold of me—
a red clawed one, a crested enemy.
I spent nine months
residing in her womb.
. . . the red-clawed one imbued me with passion.[5]

And so the shapeshifting bard has multiple lives and experiences to invoke. He knows the hunger of the roebuck for mountain herbs, the muscled gallop of stallion across the meadow. This is the source of his wisdom as well as his inspiration. In Taliesin's telling, the red-clawed Ceridwen is the source of his gift, for she gave him chase.

Here we find a deepening of Hyde's thesis, that it is trickster's appetite that motivates. For appetite is merely the surface of the more fundamental desire for life. Hunger is the symptom of vitality. The constant fight of bodies against decay, against dying, requires massive amounts of energy. So the belly reigns in the body, a tyranny of the ravenous tube.

In the end, Taliesin's own appetite for life caused him to be reborn again and again. It also caused him to be eaten himself. Taliesin thus knows that all creatures participate in this hunger for life. Herein lies his greatest inspiration: Don't go looking for wisdom unless you are ready to face the tooth and the claw. Don't go looking for a poet's tongue until you can swim the cold seas and rivers or can climb, hoof on rock, to the highest crag. Don't go feeding your own appetite until you, too, are willing to be eaten.

An organism's own bodily boundary is a process rather than a discrete thing. An amoeba's membrane denotes its affirmation of what belongs and what does not—a declaration of the self and the nonself. Boundaries can be exclusive and affirming of hierarchy, or they can denote the process of creating the contours of life. Yet the tricksters who slip through the pores open the possibility for richer life. As biologist Lynn Margulis first hypothesized, mitochondria and chloroplasts, the energy-generating organelles in animals and plants, respectively, were originally independent organisms that got swallowed up and yet partnered with their host cells.[6] These relics of past symbiosis still have their own DNA, indicating their prior independence.

And so here we see a bit of a corrective from that awkward term *autopoiesis*. Life is not just organisms constituting themselves through their own desire to continue persisting. *Sympoiesis* (a word championed by the preeminent ecofeminist,

posthumanist, and science historian Donna Haraway) cor-
rects this idea.[7] Organisms don't create themselves; rather,
they create together.

Life is a messy complex of organisms: interdependent,
undulating, interpenetrating, and hungry. Mycelium poke
into plant roots, swapping mineral for metabolite. Algae hold
hands with fungi to create a whole new species called lichen.
Bacteria slip into cells and decide to stay, trading energetic
molecules for a safehouse. Microbes hitch a ride with foods
into your ravenous intestines and settle in, happy to help break
down nutrients in exchange for regular feeding. Sympoiesis
means not just that ecosystems exist but also that you could
not exist except for the ecosystem that is your body. You are a
quivering, ravenous throng of interdependent beings.

For all the attention that food ethicists and food activists
give to what goes into our mouths, there is little consciousness
of the other end of the alimentary canal. In the same way
that the tracker looks at scat in order to more deeply understand a creature, I similarly want to look at food and appetites in reverse. What can our excrement reveal about our food
systems? Or, to use more theological language, in what ways
might poop be apocalyptic, by unveiling in colorful detail the
result of settler agriculture taken in and processed by our bellies? And how might we use this information to understand
how our hunger makes this world, for better or for worse?

In return for the chance to munch on the dregs of our din-
ners, the bacterial horde provides a host of benefits to our
bodies. A healthy gut microbiome has been correlated with
improved mood—the bacteria, it turns out, provide most of

the serotonin your brain requires to maintain levels of this happy molecule. A diverse and thriving microbiome has been linked to a healthy immune system, an array of anticancer molecules, and reduction of incidence of heart disease and diabetes.

Other important discoveries in microbiotic relationships have to do with diversity. Studies of human microbiomes (by analyzing our own scat) have shown that a greater medley of microbes impart health benefits to the hosts of these hordes. The American Gut Project, which sampled feces from more than ten thousand subjects, showed that a diet consisting of thirty or more different types of plants a week led to the most diverse microbial populations.[8]

Another analysis looked at the microbiomes of four Nepalese indigenous groups.[9] The four groups represent different food practices on a gradient from mostly foraging to long-term farming. One group, the Tharu, has been farming for more than two hundred years, while the Raute and Raji began farming approximately forty years ago. The Chepang have largely retained their hunting and gathering lifestyle. The study found that the longer a group had been farming, the less diverse their microbiome. This correlates with other studies showing that proximity in space and time to urbanization and industrialization are correlated with a decrease in the variety of biota in the belly.

So we find that human health depends on gut health, and gut health depends on an assorted and thriving population of microbial partners in our colon. Microbiomic diversity, in turn, depends on access to a diverse landscape and variety of food sources. To put it plainly, the inner ecology of your bowels depends on the biodiversity of the habitat. Your excrement, then, tells a deep story not only about your health but also about the health of the ecosystems your food lives and grows in.

Spring has arrived in Southern California. The chaparral bursts with color. Lizards lie on the edge of trails, warming their leathery bodies in the sun. Fiery orange poppies ignite the hills in a constant smokeless flame.

I sit in my backyard garden, with a grapevine trellised overhead. To my left, a lemon tree hangs with plump green ovals just beginning to yellow. To my right, a fig tree swells with large tear-shaped buds of fruit. With a knife, I cut into an avocado harvested from the tree behind me. The knife's sharp edge slips easily through the thin membrane of skin covering the soft green flesh inside. I draw the knife in an oblong circle, slicing through skin and flesh and around the large seed at the center. I grasp either side of the cut with my hands, and with a turn and pull of the wrist, the velvety thickness is exposed. I spoon out the insides and savor its rich, buttery flavor on my tongue. As I eat, I imagine the bacteria in my mouth, living their lives at the constant whim of my appetite and thirst. My sip is their flood. My taste is their feast. My hunger, their drought; my health, their well-being.

I look up to the hill called Mitsqanaqan, "Coyote's Chin," and remember: I am living in the land of the Chumash, who have lived here for millennia. Who still live here. Their ability to do so, I suspect, is because of their attention to hunger and their commitments to eat without being all-consuming.

So I bid you: eat these words. Break them down. Take them into your hungering body. Let them stir up trouble within you. May you inhabit Coyote's belly and Taliesin's tongue. May your own appetite bring flourishing to your inner and outer landscapes. May your desire make the world a more beautiful place.

INTO THE BRINE

The college I attended in Arkansas lay at the edge of the Ozark range, which covers northern Arkansas and southern Missouri and sits squarely between the Mississippi River basin to the east and the plains to the west. What our small town lacked in urban appeal it made up for with local culture. When friends and I decided to have fried catfish on a Friday night, we'd make the thirty-minute drive from our college town to the area's undisputed best catfish joint; you'd miss it if you blinked while on the road, as my grandmother might say. The draw was the freshness of the food. You had to call ahead of time to tell the cook you were coming, so that there was time to catch, clean, and gut some catfish before you got there.

Part of my lineage comes from this rugged terrain, said to be one of the places in North America that was never under the ocean in the many millennia of its history. My ancestors were relative newcomers to this old landscape. The Osage lived in the Ozarks before them and lived in the high woodlands when they were not hunting in the Great Plains. The displacement of the Osage by settler aggression and treaty opened the way for my family and others to inhabit the territory.

The mountains, valleys, hills, and hummocks are the result of the karst topography of the place. Karst landscapes—referring to the limestone geology—dissolve easily in water, giving rise to both the damp caverns and the bony bluffs the region is known for. Moreover, many of the place-names indicate the sense of mystery and even malevolent magic imbued in the region—Devil's Den, Devil's Backbone, and Devil's Tollgate are but a few of the names associating the landscape with antagonistic forces. Because of the nature of the terrain, most of the Ozark range remains fairly secluded even today. This has created a culture fairly preserved from the hubbub of history, and the people there live an existence as marginal as the thin, rocky soils they inhabit.

In Keith Basso's landmark study of the Western Apache relationship to land, *Wisdom Sits in Places*, he shows how the people use stories of their landscape to instruct each other. By attaching stories to particular places, Apache culture imbues those sites with deeper meaning and integrates them into their social identities. Consider, for instance, the witness of Nick Thompson, an elder in the Cibecue region, on the importance of story:

> So someone stalks you and tells a story about what happened long ago ... All of a sudden it hits you! It's like an arrow, they say. Sometimes it just bounces off—it's too soft and you don't think about anything. But when it's strong it goes in deep and starts working on your mind right away ... That story is

changing you now, making you want to live right. That story is
making you want to replace yourself.[1]

The term *pagan* comes from the Latin word *paganus*, meaning "of the countryside." For the Romans the term became
a diminutive, equivalent to the modern *hillbilly* or *redneck*.
Ozarkans often get called by these latter terms on account
of their culture, infused as it is with catfish, sparse living, and
regional dialect. A few years ago, in an attempt to replace
myself, I followed Nick Thompson's advice and searched out
stories from that place. These are not grand myths filled with
heroes and gods but small tales of quotidian life. The stories
seem, like water, to dissolve into the karst landscape and carry
its limestone particles and conifer-crusted soil with them. A
drink of these tales carries the subtle salty taste of the Ozarks
with it, evoked in the yokel concerns and regional words.
On reading a particular tale one evening, I was surprised to
see my own kin referenced—albeit ignominiously, as "them
spindle-assed Pritchett boys." It seems that my bloodline is
thus pagan in the truest sense, my lineage bumpkin, and the
corresponding genetic disposition of my backside apparently
spindly.

The following story came from the Ozarks.[2] It is a story as
unabashedly ribald as the mountain folk who have told it for
generations, as patriarchal as the culture they came from, and
as magical as the evening fog that sits in the valley pockets of
the rocky landscape. As a folk reflection on the erotic, this tale
speaks of loneliness, desire, fear, and ambivalence. Like Cupid,
the story carries a quiver full of arrows, and like Apache storytellers, it stalks the hearer. It shoots an arrow into the heart

of humans and their relationship to the wild. I retell it here in my own words but retain just a bit of the dialect of the hills and hollers it came from.

One time there was an old bachelor lived up on the Meramec, and he was the best noodler in the whole country. He caught more fish with his hands than most fellows could get with a big seine. He was a bit of a lonely fellow—he never did settle down with a wife, and even his friends didn't really know him. But he kept up his home pretty well on his own, and folks say he seemed happiest when he was noodling.

One evening he was feeling around in a black hole under a bunch of horsetail rushes, and a catfish mouth caught his hand and yanked it back. He hollered and pulled, but that catfish tugged back harder. With his hand caught in its mouth, he went under the water quicker than a minnow can swim a bucket, and came up sputtering and cussing. But he didn't give up—he kept rassling that catfish.

After what seemed like hours, he finally drug out a slim yellow catfish that weighed pretty near a hundred pounds. The funny thing was how that catfish kept hollering. Like one of those squealer-cats they catch out of the White River, only louder. It was still squealing when he got it home in the wagon. The rain barrel was about half full, so he just put the catfish in the barrel with its head down. He figured the water would keep it alive, and the next morning he'd sell it to the fellow that ran the new hotel in town.

During the night he heard that fish flouncing around like a mule kicking in a barn, but he knew it couldn't get away, so he just went to sleep. When he woke up, there was a woman in bed with him, naked as a plucked goose. It wasn't any of the neighbor gals; it was a plumb stranger. She was a right good-looking woman, and they stayed in bed pretty late. Finally he says, "Maybe we'd better get up"—after all, he had the farm chores to do—but the woman didn't seem to have any clothes, so he didn't mention it anymore. After a while he went outside and saw that the big catfish was gone from the rain barrel. It looked like a lot of funny things were happening. The bachelor thought maybe he was going crazy, but he didn't say anything. He just went back to the house and crawled back in bed.

So that's how things went for three whole weeks, and the bachelor was plumb wore down to a nub. It wasn't that he was hungry—he hadn't been since she had arrived in his bed. It wasn't the smell either. He never did have much reason to bathe that often, and his hands often smelled of fish on account of his occupation. He just plain wanted his old life back. His homestead was falling to pieces.

But whenever he got to thinking about some way to get rid of the woman, she would just look at him. She never said a word, only just looked at him and went right ahead with what she was doing. Some women is awful single-minded, and it looked like there was the Devil to pay and no pitch too hot. The old bachelor felt pretty bad, and haggard besides. Everything was going plumb to hell, and he knew the weeds were taking over the whole place, but there was no help for it.

One morning he woke up before daylight and the woman was gone. He figured she must have gone outdoors for a minute, so he just lay there and tried to think. Maybe he'd leave the whole goddamn country and go to Oklahoma or somewhere out west. Pretty soon he heard something floundering outside like a mule kicking in the barn. When he looked out the door, he saw that slim yellow catfish in the rain barrel, tail flapping against the clapboards.

Soon as he saw that fish, the old bachelor ran for the barn. He hitched up faster than the boys at the fire station, got that barrel in the wagon, and leaped in the front seat. Down the lane they went, with the mules at full gallop and water splashing every which way. You'd have thought he was making his way to town to sell that catfish, but instead he headed toward the river. Soon as he came to deep water, the old bachelor turned the barrel sideways, and that catfish slid head-first down the bank and into the river. The big fish turned around and looked at him just once, then twisted away, flipping her tail and diving into the murky water. That was the last he saw of her.

That old bachelor never did eat fish anymore, and he never noodled anymore either. He used to tell people that anything that smelled of fish made him sick nowadays. But folks say he walks down to the edge of that river fairly often, particular in the spring, and he'll sit on that bank for hours, just looking at a black hole under the horsetail rushes.

This is a story about the antipathy between wildness and domestication, and the erotic ecology that sits in the middle of these themes. An unresolved tension in the Ozark story revolves around just who is trapped and in bondage. On the one hand, the narrator seems to indicate that the bachelor feels trapped by the catfish woman. Her erotic embrace appears inescapable, as if he is in bondage. On the other hand, one could argue that the catfish woman is captive and that the bachelor has the power. After all, he's the one who pulled her out of the river and threw her into a barrel. He was going to sell her to be gutted and fried. Perhaps she didn't even want the amorous encounter but instead used it as a mechanism of survival.

A common trope in mythology is the affinity between wildness and femininity, both associated as they are with fertility. It would be remiss to discuss this relationship without noting that both have been abused by patriarchal power systems for millennia. Wendell Berry observes that societies tend to treat their land the same way they treat women.[3] Sylvia Federicci puts it more sharply: in parallel development with the closing of public commons in Europe in the fifteenth through eighteenth centuries was the simultaneous removal of women's economic and social agency.[4] Women were pushed out of trade guilds and marginalized to the lowest-paid menial labor, while protections against abuse such as rape were lifted. When public lands were privatized, women's bodies became the new commons. Thus, patriarchal civilizations have viewed women and the wild in the same way: as fertile resources to be managed and controlled. Given this link—even with its attendant and problematic norms—this tale of the bachelor, the catfish, and the riverbank has much to say about our attraction to and ambivalence about the wild.

The story appears to be a variant of a much older Welsh story adapted to the Ozark context.[5] In the tale from South Wales, the fish caught is a salmon. The character of salmon woman rather than the fisher drives that story, and the plot revolves more around her and her desires. In fact, when the boy who caught her refuses her advances in the boat, she intentionally capsizes it and nearly drowns him until he agrees to marry her. He then uses his knife to remove the hook in her lip, and afterward she kisses him and uses her blood on his face to cast a spell on him: "Now thou has taken of my blood thou wilt love me forever." And of course, as is the case with these sorts of stories, they did live happily and have many children—all of whom had a slight scar on their lips.

Hillbilly bards in the Ozarks traded the elegant salmon in the Welsh version for the culturally disdained catfish. Catfish are known as bottom-feeders, a species that will eat nearly anything—when fishing, the stinkier the bait, the better. Nevertheless, catfish have been an important source of food in the Ozarks and other places across the globe. They are said to grow indefinitely, as long as there is food and space available—I have met someone whose job was to dive in dams to check for structural soundness, and he swears he saw a catfish at the bottom of a dam the size of a small car. This is not completely outlandish. A catfish was caught in Thailand with a confirmed weight of 646 pounds. Most consider the catfish appearance grotesque, their barbels (whiskers) contributing to this general sense. But the catfish is a perfect choice for this allegorical story. Catfish do not have scales—they are naked, so to speak—and their thin skin is covered in gustatory and olfactory nerve endings. In short, the catfish is a naked animal that can touch, taste, and smell with every part of its body. A catfish person would therefore have a remarkable capacity for bawdy behavior.

The Ozark story, in contrast to the Welsh one, focuses on the male bachelor as protagonist. In keeping with traditional culture, he makes his living by several means, but the story indicates that his primary mode of both subsistence and income is by catching catfish. Noodling, or "noodlin'" in local parlance, refers to the tradition of catching catfish by standing in a creek or river and putting one's hand in a catfish hole and wiggling one's fingers. When the catfish tries to eat the fingers, the noodler can grab the fish by its mouth and pull it out of its lair and into a boat. This form of fishing is somewhat dangerous both because a large catfish can allegedly wrestle a noodler under water and because there likely are snakes in the river.

The noodling bachelor of our story is thus a man accustomed to danger, a person who lives on the periphery of civilization and the wild river. By virtue of his livelihood, he has not been completely swallowed up by culture. He thrives on that muddy riparian transition zone of the riverbank, where land and water meet, and, like the archetype of the hunter, seems at home in the places human culture has not conquered. Moreover, he echoes the archetype of the fisher-king of the grail legend, whose chronic wound was relieved of pain only when he was fishing. The bachelor's wound is not explicitly named in the tale, just inferred. His existence at the edge of the land and water is literally marginal. He subsists on his day labor of fishing and depends on his angler acumen in order to survive. He is lonely, says the narrator, but it is unclear whether he abandoned society or the town isolated him. Either way, he seems to have some feral qualities.

Gary Snyder defines wildness in animals and plants as being "free agents, self-propagating, flourishing in accord with their innate properties,"[6] which fits remarkably well with Audre Lorde's sense of how erotic power liberates women—and perhaps all people—to live by their deepest understanding of themselves: "Our erotic knowledge empowers us, becomes the lens we scrutinize all aspects of our existence through, forcing us to evaluate those aspects honestly in terms of their relative meaning in our lives."[7]

Yet the story tells us that as wild as he is in comparison to the townsfolk, the bachelor still cannot handle the amorous appetite of the catfish woman. When they finally meet, she pulls him into the water—baptizes him—and the rest of the story hinges on whether he might live in accordance with that baptism or forsake it and her. She beckons him to bed while he desires to get up and do the chores, to maintain his connection to civilization by having a proper homestead, maintained against the constant entropy of nature and insistence of the weeds. Perhaps he cannot imagine a life fulfilled by anything other than his proximity to the town and its culture, even her amorous company. On the other hand, he may have known that when the erotic comes home, it is no longer exotic but mundane, and he refused to integrate his fantasy into the quotidian routine of his existence. The bachelor of the Ozark tale glimpsed the power of Eros in his encounter with the catfish woman, yet rather than being freed to live more fully, he was afraid of this erotic power—not of the catfish woman in his bed but of his deep self. Lorde gives voice to that fear: "We have been raised to fear the yes within ourselves, our deepest cravings . . . but when we begin to live from within outward, in touch with the power of the erotic within ourselves, and allowing that power to inform and illuminate our actions upon the world around us, then we begin to be responsible to ourselves in the deepest sense."[8]

Erotic power is thus a way to describe a condition of wildness and liberation from social constraints that prevent humans from living fully into their potential.

For too long, desire and sensuality have been maligned. Depicted as base or sinful throughout much of Christianity's heyday, the erotic was seen as an instinct that was corrupt. On the other hand, in Ancient Mesopotamia, it seems that sexuality was a quality that separated humans from the natural world. In the Epic of Gilgamesh, one of the oldest recorded myths, the wild Enkidu is tamed by the ministrations of a temple prostitute. Enkidu, who would later become the companion of Gilgamesh, king of Uruk, is created by the gods as a feral man. He runs the mountains like a goat. He eats grasses like gazelles. He jostles the other animals at the watering hole. He destroys the traps of a hunter. According to the story, this hunter tells Gilgamesh of a fearsome wild man whose body is covered in shaggy hair, and Gilgamesh sends the prostitute Shamhat to tame him. After spending two weeks in the embrace of Shamhat, Enkidu leaves the watering hole for civilization, and eventually meets Gilgamesh.

And so, for the writers of the epic, sexuality seems to be associated with civilization. Enkidu's erotic encounter brings him away from the jostling community of creatures at the watering hole. The task, it seems, is to rewrite the epic within ourselves. We must reject the notion from Gilgamesh and the thousands of years after it that our erotic power separates us from the watering hole. We must also put away notions that desire is corrupt.

Andreas Weber notes that the liberatory power of erotic self-awareness is not limited to describing human relationships.

Erotic encounter is the fundamental way to experience the entire world we are embedded in. We are always enveloped in musty clouds of air, full of the molecules of oxygen exhaled by trees, the shed dead cells of other animals, floating bacteria, mycelial spores, and pollen, the very *sperma* (Greek for "seed") of plants. The Krebs cycle, that crux of biology so many had to memorize in school, also reveals the interconnectedness of our bodies with their environments. A short lesson in biochemistry reminds us of the importance of this foundational chemical reaction. When our bodies break down sugars, the cycle yields by-products of adenosine triphosphate (usable energy) and carbon dioxide. The significance of the carbon dioxide by-product is that it comes not from the food we ingest but, rather, from our own bodies. *Metabolism* comes from a Greek word that means "change," and indeed the Krebs cycle shows that our bodies are constantly in flux, taking in molecules from the air, from our food, and cycling them through our bodies, simultaneously shedding cells and molecules. We live ever in relationship.

To study biology is to become aware that the world is full of the eros of life engaged with life. This erotic power, which Weber calls *enlivenment*, pervades our lives:

> No biological description is complete unless it is laid out as
> a biology of love. And conversely, we do not understand love
> if we fail to see that it is linked to the living world, to the
> experience of inhabiting a living body that trembles in joy and
> winces in pain. Love is a practice of enlivenment. The erotic
> is the genuine principle of life that permeates the world of
> bodies and life-forms.[9]

Enlivenment, as defined by Weber, enables us to understand our life-places as full of erotic potential. As animals full of such potential, Weber suggests we practice an *erotic ecology*, that is, a relationship to place characterized by the deep joy of self-knowledge always already in relationship with the constant caress of the teeming web of life around us. That web is not just around us, a stewing soup we swim in, but also within; the body is a biome, the intestines a hothouse for belching bacteria, skin a layered landscape of nooks and crannies for microbes living in a mutual arrangement with our flesh.

Whatever the reason, in the end of the story, the canoodling noodler trades life with the catfish woman for civilization. He even gives up fishing as part of his livelihood. But the story holds whispering hints that he regrets his decision. That black catfish hole under the horsetail rushes was his doorway to deeper connection. He had spent his life on the margins, and when given the chance to dive deeper into connection with the water and the wild, he spurned his yearning for the sake of the security of the known life. He is Jacob wrestling God, and he is the Grail king—but his limp is his loneliness, and his wound is his awareness of having been offered enlivenment, and trading it instead for dull daily talk of weather in the town square and froth at the bottom of his beer pint in the tavern.

It may be that the story we need is one with a more insistent fish woman, such as the salmon woman in the Welsh tale. And if the predictions of climatologists have it right, we may very well be half-drowned by the wild—just as the Welsh fisher-boy was—before we agree to be its lover. Yet the Ozark story is remarkable precisely because that catfish woman is not insistent; she does not attempt to convince the bachelor of anything. She dunks him in the muddy baptismal waters of her river but does not force him to consent to partnership. Rather, she merely gives him what she has to offer, and he is forced to make a choice.

The question before him is whether he will live into that floundering, struggling baptism on the banks of the Merimac. Baptism brings the possibility of newness to the bachelor, not by more of the tired old dogma found in the halls of hill country church houses but as an entree to an enlivened existence. That old Ozark bachelor got an intimate encounter with the erotic wild, and so might we, through the skin-caressing waters of baptism.

Why speak of baptism, in a time of rising seas and changing shorelines? Why a sacrament, when religion has in so many ways, for so long, proved itself the very antithesis of holding life sacred? Because ritual bathing is such an ancient, global, and sensual act, from the Ganges to the Jordan. Because, as the Lakota have recently reminded settlers in North America, water is life.[10] Because, as Irish poet John O'Donohue, tells us, water is our first mother, "vehicle and idiom of all the inner voyaging that keeps us alive."[11]

The meaning of baptism as a doorway to the erotic edges of existence is evident in a text by the Greek physician Nicander, who lived in the second century BCE. The Greek word *baptizo* occurs in a passage in which he describes how to make pickles.[12] First, says Nicander, you dip the vegetables in a hot-water bath. But this is not baptism; he uses a related word, *bapto*, to describe this act that is temporally shorter. No, *baptizo*, says

Nicander, is what happens when you submerge a vegetable to be pickled. It has to simmer awhile in that murky, fermenting brine. When that vegetable comes out, it's a pickle, changed by the alchemy of that bubbling broth. Baptism as practice, then, reminds us that life fundamentally consists of erotic interpenetration and embrace of the wriggling bodies of the world.

Theologian Ched Myers observes that when Jesus was baptized in the Jordan River, he was immersed, in some sense, into the entire Jordan River watershed.[13] In a watershed, rainwater flows from the high points across the landscape and runs into the river, gathered by gravity. If water unites all the creatures in a watershed by its flow across the landscape, the river symbolizes that community of creatures bound together by water.

It is no accident, then, that John the Baptist, cousin of Jesus, chose the Jordan River as the location for his work. The river was a synecdoche for the land community of the entire watershed, as well as allegory for a new possibility of living in the land, just as when the Hebrews first crossed the Jordan into the promised land. The text gives the sense that the wild man John was catfish-like himself, undoubtedly whiskered and with a fondness for locusts. The gospel of Mark says that John was preaching a baptism of repentance and for the forgiveness of sins: in the Greek text, *metanoia* and release of *hamartia*.[14] Centuries of Western doctrine have muddled the meaning of these words, but Apache elder Nick Thompson's discussion of the function of place-based story sheds light on the prophetic work of that feral prophet John. First, *metanoia*, "to change one's mind," takes on a richer meaning in light of what Thompson reveals. Stories are like arrows, he says, that "work on your mind . . . changing you now, making you want to live right" in relation to the places they describe. The Greek word *hamartia* originally meant "to miss the mark," referring to an arrow having missed its target. Western fetishism of the binary logic of right and wrong, good and evil, truth and lie has clouded the important part of this metaphor. The problem is not that the arrow did not hit the target; rather, when it misses the mark, the arrow cannot do what it was meant to do—it cannot, in Thompson's words, make you want to *replace* yourself. To replace oneself, in his worldview, is to live according to the rhythmic patterns of the local context, to inhabit rightly the bioregion to which the human community belongs. The elder concedes that often the problem is not that the arrow story misses the mark but, rather, that it is not sharp enough or strong enough to stay in the target, to penetrate deeply and cause *metanoia*. A dull or weakly shot arrow can bounce off, and so can shallow stories.

The desert proclamations of John were thus not about a narrowly conceived forgiveness of individual sins; rather, they were about transforming a people too accustomed to shallow imperial stories. His sharp words struck deep and made people want to live right. His arrow-stories and prophet-conjuring preaching provoked the denizens of Judea to replace themselves, starting with immersion back into their ancestral river, steeped as it was with silty sediment.

Would you be baptized in your local river? When I lived in the rural Midwest, heartland of industrial agriculture, warnings were issued after rains that the local river was toxic, contaminated as it was by coliform bacteria, nitrogen, and phosphates spread across the land. A dip in the water on a hot day was no chlorinated christening in a sanitized sanctuary, but a turbid plunge into the whole of the watershed. That water had coalesced from the uppermost reaches of the watershed, first in trickles, then in streams, and finally cascading into the steeper banks of the river. That same water rushing by our submerged bodies had moved across grassy fields and passed through the beating hearts of mammals, carrying with it the excrement of animals and sediment of soils.

Baptism is thus no cleansing of microbial life, dirt, and salt from our skin; instead it is a bath of brine. It brings us deeper into the life of the world by caressing our bodies with this teeming soup, by immersing us into an erotic ecology.

Ritual immersion into the pollution and promise of the watershed symbolizes this connection to its creatures. Plunging into murky waters contaminated by bacterial and industrial effluent depends on a willingness to inhabit the world as it is and as we have made it. To be reborn is not to *leave* the world and all its contingency but to *return* to the ever-brewing fecundity of the earth. Rebirth is a transforming and replacing of the self.

Baptism as a call *into* deeper conviviality with other creatures— the old stories remind us—must also be a call *out of* the civilization that holds us back from fully inhabiting our bodies and our homeplaces as free, enlivened beings. In other words, our ecosystems might become our allies in the liberation of our bodies. This is reflected in the long association of baptism with the story of the Israelite exit from the Egyptian empire. Central to the escape was the crossing of the Red Sea:

a submersive, subversive evasion from an enemy army out of which the ex-slaves emerged into wilderness.

The Red Sea was called "a sea of reeds"—a reference to the water plants growing in it, which indicate slow-moving, shallow, muddy waters. This ecotone (the meeting of two ecosystems, in this case land and water) was a perfect ally for a people on the run. Such swamplands are ecological zones of abundance. One measure of abundance is net primary productivity, a measure of the amount of energy produced by life-forms in a given ecosystem. Net primary productivity in wetlands is one of the highest on earth, matched only by tropical rain forests. That ubiquitous energy gets converted into food for the many organisms brimming in the water.

I experienced this productivity of wetlands firsthand in— of all places—the arid Southwest. I was on a desert survival course, on the second day without food as the cohort I traveled with scavenged the landscape looking for water and nutrition. By the afternoon of our second day hiking multiple miles without substantial calorie sources, we were all tired and hungry, ready for anything that would fuel our movement across the rocky landscape. When we walked near a thicket of willows, a sure sign of water, one companion slipped through the bushy hedge and exclaimed, "Cattails!" In response our band fought through the foliage and began to sink into soaked ground. We had chanced upon a spring-fed wetland, full of cattails and bubbling, smelly water.

A few of us waded carefully into the warm bog, stepping on floating islands of vegetation to keep from sinking too deeply. The water felt warm, as swamp water often does: the constant fermenting action of the denizens digesting their way through the organic matter heats it. As I moved gingerly across vegetal islands, a course instructor reached down into the muck and pulled a thick cattail up from the root. Cattails have long been a significant source of starchy carbohydrate, and we all sampled the root. The slimy exterior easily pulled away, exposing the white root flesh underneath. We all sampled a few roots, hungry but careful not to overharvest this precious resource. The crunch was refreshing and mildly sweet, and gave me extra energy to continue to hike throughout the day. While my exposure to this abundance found in a bog was in the context of a guided survival course, I could easily imagine the importance of wetland abundance to cultures that depend on their landscape for sustenance.

Thus, whereas the state apparatus of Egypt attempted control of food and management of population, the reedy sea was a dip into a realm of abundant life-processes and unfettered fecundity. Passing through the marshy muck prepared those Hebrew refugees to inhabit new lifeways in the wilderness, away from the brick and mortar mundanity of the empire they left.

Elsewhere, too, wetlands have served as an escape ecology. Osceola led the Seminoles to successfully evade the US army for years in the Florida Everglades. In the sixth century CE, the historian Procopius wrote that Slavs escaped the invading army of emperor Justinian by hiding out in the Pripet marshes of Eastern Europe.

The Mesopotamian marshlands have long been known as a refuge for people on the run from empires even in the days of the Sumerian city-states. British explorer Wilfred Thesiger hypothesized that the marshes, "with their baffling maze of reed-beds where men could move only by boat, must have afforded a refuge to remnants of a defeated people and been a centre for lawlessness and rebellion since the earliest times."[15] For instance, the Zanj rebellion against the Abbasid caliphate in the ninth century CE utilized the marshy maze as a refuge from the military of the caliphate. This revolt consisted of both East African slaves as well as Arabs who were able to wage a fourteen-year war, partially due to their ability to hide guerrilla style in the marshes between attacks.

State-maintained cultures around the world have developed binary terms to compare themselves to the irrepressible populations evading their control. Many of these are still used in everyday language: civilized versus wild, tame and feral, hill folk and valley folk, country and city, Christian and savage. This way of speaking creates a dichotomy in which one side is assumed superior and dehumanizes the other, in contradiction to lived experience.

James C. Scott notes a particularly vivid metaphorical binary used by the Chinese. They describe hill-dwelling people who have shirked state culture as "raw," as opposed to their civilized, "cooked" culture.[16] This metaphor retains all the trappings of civilizational hubris: state-dwelling citizens have a diet full of cooked grains, which they viewed as cultured in relation to their hillbilly neighbors, whose palate is rich in an abundance of foraged plants, hunted game, and supplemented with small patches of cultivated root vegetables. However, as Scott notes, the lowlanders' grain-based diet is subject to taxation and theft; grains and pulses like rice and beans are harvested at certain times and stored, making it administratively simple for states to take portions. Hills and their ecosystems do not typically lend themselves to cultivation of grains and pulses, so people living in mountainous ecosystems utilize a larger variety of food—often foraged and hunted. If they do have cultivated systems, these usually consist of tree crops or root crops left in the ground or on the tree until needed. Thus, we might see the ecosystem itself as supporting an anti-imperial diet by limiting the type of cultivation possible.

The ritual of baptism still retains these seeds of liberation underlined by erotic encounter with the wild. It may not be possible to go from "cooked" back to "raw"—there is no straight line backward from our industrial predicament to a more whole and intimate relationship to the land—but perhaps we can go from cooked to fermented, becoming pickled by baptism. To do so, we will have to be willing to face the brackish waters our culture has created: the Pacific Garbage Patch, the dead zone of the Gulf of Mexico, the many brownfields and Superfund sites at the banks of our rivers and streams already brimming from upstream pesticides and herbicides. Behind these noxious waters lie millennia of dominance of women's bodies, wealth accumulation through slavery and expropriation of lands, and religious monocultures that serve state interests. Civilization has bartered stories like arrows for blunted narratives that serve conquest for centuries.

But in those waters still resides a simmering alchemy of microbial life. Even now, billions of bacteria are slowly digesting the plastics in the Pacific Garbage Patch and converting them back into organic life. Even now, indigenous people rise up, as they always have, against continued colonization. Even now, women resist patriarchal attempts to control their bodies, people of the African diaspora resurrect their insistence that their lives matter in the face of state-sanctioned killings of black bodies. The briny bath of baptism invites us to dive more deeply into an erotic ecology, a greater camaraderie with the creatures inhabiting our watersheds, and perhaps an escape from imperial ways of living in the world. Life is fermenting and fomenting all around.

If we are willing to plunge into the water and into the wild, practicing an erotic, liberating relationship to the land community, we may yet find our way home. A slim yellow catfish waits in the water; maroons and mossbacks sit against the trunks of the cypress; wild-haired John wades through knee-high waters beckoning us to join him for a dip. Somewhere in the deep, a creature turns in the muck, and bubbles slowly rise to the surface.

Welcome to the fellowship of the fermented.

THE TREE, THE AX, AND
THE STRUGGLE FOR LIFE

I pause, kneeling before the trunk. It is still a young tree—the base is only as big around as my thigh. Cutting down a tree seems such an act of violence in this age of rampant fires and widespread logging. How much carbon will this release into the atmosphere? What would I feel if I could hear the chemical screams released by the dying foliage? But this pear tree was planted too close to another and has struggled to live. The few scattered fruits hang limply from unpruned branches, dried on the limb like mummified pendants displayed for this macabre decapitation.

For the health of this backyard forest, the tree must go. The size of the trunk hardly merits an ax, but this is the only tool I have. One swing sinks the ax head solidly into the base. Bark chips fly off easily, betraying the dehydration of the fibers and illness of the tree. The sharpness of the new ax makes the work easy, and soon with a push and a crack the tree falls. I save what I can for fires and cut the stump low to the ground.

Some stories ring so tragic that they must continue to be told. Sometimes a tragedy becomes a metaphor for itself.

It happened like this. A tree, the Tree of Ténéré, grew in the Sahara. Originally this hardy tree was part of a stand of acacias that grew in the area during a wetter climate period. Over time the rest of the trees died out, but this lonely acacia continued to survive due to roots that reached over a hundred feet deep into the water table. This tree, the only one for hundreds of miles, was known by the nomadic Tuareg and was a landmark for journeys across the expansive desert. Nomads revered the tree, and no animal or human harmed the leaves or branches. Some even called it sacred.

Early maps made by European colonizers featured the tree. Twentieth-century French explorers mentioned it in the details of their expeditions. Ethnologist Henri Lhote came upon it in his travels and said that although it looked sick or ill, it had nice green leaves and even yellow flowers. A French military commander, Michel Lesourd, after seeing the remarkable tree in 1939, wrote that it was a "living lighthouse" for caravans crossing this region of the desert. "One must see the tree to believe its existence," he wrote.[1]

But after Lhote returned to the site twenty-five years later, he mourned its appearance: "Before, this tree was green and with flowers; now, it is a colorless thorn tree and naked." A truck driver passing the tree on his route had crashed into it.

Improbably, the tree survived being hit by a vehicle that damaged one of its two stems. Then, in 1973, an allegedly drunk driver struck it again. The second wound was mortal, and the dead trunk of the tree now resides in the Niger National Museum. Rumbling machines hit the only tree for hundreds of miles not once but twice, and now a metal statue of a tree stands in its place in memory.

When was the first story told? Was it around a fire, or under a tree? Did it induce dread or praise? Was it spoken or sung from the lips of the first bards? Did the spoken words plow acres in the heart? We will never know the first story, but we do know old stories. Their age is not branded on their thighs; rather, it is inferred by the moss dripping from their branching words and the deep grooves in the trunk of their narratives.

This is an old story, one that arose after humans first began to build fires so hot that they melted metal out of stone. The bards of great lodges hammered the edges of this tale year after year, until its sharpness cut words of warning into the hearer, cautioning that those who fashioned weapons could not be entirely trusted. This is a story about the first blacksmith. The story is told in many places across the world and is considered one of the oldest fairy tales known.[2] The version below is my own telling.

See a man walking. This is a man sent from his village. He walks away with his head down. He walks shamefaced. He did the unspeakable, and reconciliation is impossible. He recalls the disclosure, the council, the banishment.

Each step carries him farther from parents, village festivals, dances around fires, and the many hands that fed him as he grew from teetering toddler to headstrong teenager to now disgraced man. Every rock he passes is a wall between himself and belonging. He walks until the road becomes a path, then a trail, and finally dissolves to an animal run before petering out into a rocky plain.

As dusk turns to black night, he decides to stop at an alcove in a bluff beside him. With cold hands, he gathers kindling. He reflects on the dead branches, cut off, like him, from the sap that nourished them. He resolves to build a large fire—perhaps because his heart feels cold, perhaps to fend off howling beasts, and perhaps because he wants to burn away his loneliness.

Night deepens on this solitary human, and raging fire dims to glowing bed of coals. As he drifts into sleep, a noise startles him, and he sits up from his makeshift bed of evergreen branches. A figure appears from the distant shadows, suddenly, like the pop of stars into the night sky. The man puts a hand on his bone knife and asks the stranger who he is. Now the stranger is in the red light of the coals. His face looks at once as young as that of a baby emerging from the womb and yet as old as rocks washed up from the sea, his eyes match the coals' red glow, and his hands extending from his cloak look charred, like the upper branches of a tree after a wildfire. The former villager has never met this shadowed figure but knows he has many names, the first of which is Devil.

The devil pulls out a blade, the likes of which the outcast man has never seen. It is an impossibly thin mineral, shaped to an impossibly sharp edge. The devil tosses it beside the wary man, inviting him to take it in his hands, to admire the angle of the blade, its strength and contour. As the man wonders at this marvel, he imagines the power this could give him. It is lighter than stone yet stronger than bone. Its durability would cut in half the hours spent sharpening his antelope-bone edge, and this blade would last a thousand times longer than his. Though it seems like magic to the man, the devil calls it metal and says it is a magic that can be replicated. As his mind travels in possibilities, the devil makes an offer. He will teach the man how to make this and many more marvels out of the very rock surrounding them and the hot coals between them. But as is the case in these old stories, there must always be an exchange. In return for teaching this metallurgic magic, the man must give the devil his soul.

The man looks into the stewing coals of the fire and thinks of his future. He sees a bare existence, by day finding food, and night by lonely night fitful sleep alongside coals such as these. He cannot walk far enough to find a village that would take him; the entire region knows of his banishment. He is not afraid of the forest or the animals; he is afraid of losing the songs of the clan. What is a soul without a village anyway? What is life without a tribe?

He looks up at this strange devil and quietly assents to the proposition. A close-lipped smile cuts across the devil's face, curved like the blade he gave the man. Lessons start at once, as the devil shows the man how to find veins of metal in the rock, how to build a coal bed hot enough to smelt the ore from rock. The man soon finds a deeper cave in the bluff, where he is protected from wind and rain and his coals can burn always. He learns that the fire of his forge nourishes him, and he needs neither food nor sleep. The devil visits often, showing the man new techniques, and new implements. Soon the man's cave fills with knives, then axes, then swords.

The devil names him Smith. After a time the smoke from
Smith's perpetual fire blackens his skin: his arms and hands
look as charred as the devil's. This work is hard, and his shoulders, arms, and torso harden from the long hours of swinging
hammer and lifting rock and metal as he pounds alloy into
allegiance. The din of metal replaces his yearning for village
song, the percussive power of his blows dim his anger.

Smith longs to take his knowledge back to his community.
He no longer aches for his people or their gods—the hammer
is now his handshake, and tongs have replaced the clasping of
his hands in prayer. But he is confident that this new technology would reconcile him to the village and even leverage him
into a position of authority. His attempts to leave, however,
are thwarted by the devil.

Once, he tries to leave in the night with nothing but a small
bag of his goods. But despite his careful footsteps, he looks up
to see the cloaked figure with the curved-blade smile standing
in front of him, asking if he has forgotten the deal. After a
dozen more unsuccessful attempts to leave, each met by the
devil with prescience and contempt, the blacksmith develops
a plan:

> See this blacksmith at his forge;
> he is conjuring something new.
> Watch him coax hot coals
> out of fat logs of wood. Feel the heat
> of his furnace as he squeezes
> glowing metal from the veins of the rock.
> Hear the clanging as he beats

the yielding mineral, the hiss of steam
as he dips it into water. Smell the alchemy
of fire, water, and earth as the blacksmith
molds cuffs onto the chains he has created.

The old bards don't tell us how he did it, just that he did. Smith tricks the devil and fastens him to the chains affixed to the rock wall of the cave. He forces the devil to renege on the agreement; the maker of chains is no longer enslaved.

The blacksmith leaves his cave to return to the village. When he arrives at the gate, there is no one left who remembers who he is. Smith does not know how long he was gone, only that he now has a kind of magic that gives him and his people great advantage in the land. The power of his anvil is indeed mighty and shapes the course of civilization. His story is told around fires, but only when the flame has dimmed to the red glow of coals, and only in hushed whispers when the town blacksmith has gone to sleep. When they hear of his story, the enslaved ones crouching in iron chains or peering out with hands wrapped around steel bars always wonder whether he did indeed get his soul back from the devil.

Some mythmakers, bards, and storytellers traded love of words for love of power. Their tongues, once free to fly across the land singing songs that made people feel alive, were constrained to tell stories that bound people to a king. Where formerly the bards looked in the tracks of beetles to find stories of the stars, they now sought the glitter of gold to inspire tales of triumph.

Story itself became captured. Words were bound by the technology of writing. On stone and clay, stories once as fleetingly beautiful as the sunset were dissected and preserved. Once in service to the community, they now promoted the interests of the king. Stories were no longer the gift of a teller possessed by the spirit of the songbird but the result of tedious machinations of tired scribes waiting on their bowl of barley.

Kings of old empires knew this: if a tale can move a people to love or hate, a myth can make a nation.

One of the oldest myths recorded in writing is the Epic of Gilgamesh. This story relates the adventures of Gilgamesh, a Sumerian king. Gilgamesh the king was a despot, known for his unmatched ability in battle and his insistence on his right of first night—that is, his right to rape any bride the first night of her marriage. This, along with his boasting, led the Sumerian gods to see him as a problem. They create Enkidu, a wild man, to best Gilgamesh and dethrone him.

The epic is self-aware of its wrestling with humans and their relationship to wildness: in the second tablet, Gilgamesh encounters Enkidu and the two begin to fight. After Enkidu acknowledges Gilgamesh's superior strength, the two become friends. It is the episode after this, though, that speaks most clearly to the fraught relationship between civilization and the wild.

Gilgamesh and his friend Enkidu decide to embark on a mission to slay Huwawa, the god of the forest, and cut down his stand of great cedars. As they approach the cedar forest, Gilgamesh's nightly dreams foreshadow his victory. In a tablet discovered in 2011, newly found verses portray Huwawa less as a terrible ogre and more as the guardian of a beautiful domain.[3] Huwawa takes daily walks through his forest on a well-trodden path. The cedars offer fragrance and delight, and a chorus of monkeys, cicadas, and birds sing for their forest god. In addition, fragmented lines seem to indicate that Huwawa knew Enkidu from his earlier days as an undomesticated man, adding betrayal to injury.

When Huwawa comes out of his stronghold to fight, the god Shamash aids Gilgamesh by sending strong winds to bind Huwawa. Gilgamesh and Enkidu start felling cedars, and with each cut, Huwawa loses strength. Advancing up the mountain and continuing the clear-cut, finally they reach the paralyzed Huwawa. Gilgamesh and Enkidu spend a moment deliberating whether they should kill this guardian of the forest. They decide to do so, and when they cut off his head in the same way they chopped down the cedars, the forest trembles and the mountains quake. After slaying Huwawa, Enkidu appears remorseful, stating, "We have reduced the forest to a wasteland." But this regret lasts only a moment. They then commence with beheading the cedars just as they had Huwawa.

Babylon remembers its heroes as the ones who take up the blacksmith's implements not only against each other but also against nature herself.

The Epic of Gilgamesh leaves the fate of the trees with the episode of Huwawa, but the forged ax continued its hungry march through the cedared forests of history.

Axes are simple machines, made to reduce the amount of effort needed to slice and separate the wood or substrate being chopped. The earliest hand ax, made of stone flaked to an ax shape and held by hand, is an estimated 3.6 million years old. Stone tools like this lie buried about the globe and represent some of the most common evidence of early humanoid activity. Ax-making technology became more complex as the stone edges were ground to finer points. Then metal technology—first with copper, then bronze, and finally iron and steel—vastly improved the efficiency of these chopping machines. Ax work is not a nuanced craft, but rough, and the tool itself is intended for speed and efficiency rather than finesse. Stone axes could certainly bring down trees, but the hard, sharp edge of metal axes allowed people to do so with less effort and quicker results.

A direct relationship developed between metallurgy and deforestation. Blacksmithing technology required much fuel to burn for the shaping of alloys, so as civilizations needed more axes, blades, and other metal tools, more trees were sacrificed at the altar of the forge. At the same time, the ax allowed for quicker clearance of forest for farmland, or, as in the case of Gilgamesh, for building cities for growing populations.

This story happened over and over. As upland deforestation led to siltation of the plains between the Tigris and Euphrates, the Fertile Crescent was cleared and plowed into desert. In Greece, Plato mourned the "skeleton of the land left" on the peninsula, once full of large forests. The Greek historian Strabo blamed the deforestation of Cyprus on copper mines and shipbuilding, while the Roman historian Lucretius wrote in the first century BCE that farmers daily "constrain the woods more and more to reside up the mountains, and to give up the land beneath to tilth."[4] Homer described timber clearing as sounding like a battle. Even the peacenik passage of the prophet Isaiah, urging swords to be beat into plowshares, merely traded war against humans for war against the earth, as the plow blade cut through roots and mycelia that gave strength and fertility to the soil. In the place now called Turkey, centuries of upland deforestation led to the deposition of soil at ports and harbors, leading seaside cities to abandon their sites and move downstream as the coast moved farther and farther away from them.

The first millennium CE saw rising populations in Europe continue deforestation. An early Anglo-Saxon poet described the farmer as "grey foe of the woods,"[5] doubtless due to the constant clearing of woods for more agricultural land. Religious establishments and lords encouraged increases in new settlements and farmland throughout Western Europe. One researcher, Roland Bechmann, showed that forests in France were reduced by 66 percent between 800 and 1300 CE.[6] Eastern Orthodox settlers expanded into the forests of Russia, hanging side by side the icon and the ax, both indicating a security for peasants—the former demonstrating surety of faith, and the latter representing confidence in their ability to conquer the dark woods.[7] The Islamic empire, which originated in the arid and wood-poor areas of the Middle East, opened new lumber sources for shipbuilding and wood-based goods after conquering Spain and Sicily.

By the sixteenth century Western Europe experienced enough local wood shortages that national concerns developed. A conglomerate of timber needs—for charcoal, fuelwood, agricultural land, building material—along with lack of replanting forced many villages to source wood farther and farther away. The reign of Elizabeth I saw the first English commission to study timber decline, and this led to a series of investigations on the matter, as well as laws prohibiting or restricting woodcutting in the countryside. For governments, the pressure of scarcity related to shipbuilding. A large warship required up to two thousand oaks at least a hundred years old. The proverb of Englishman Arthur Standish, "No wood no kingdome," rang true as the imperialism of the age required a strong navy to control trade on the seas.[8]

Later the European invasion of the Americas brought the ax to a new continent. A host of factors led to the colonial expansion in the Americas, but certainly the recognition of the vast resources on the continent encouraged the rapid settlement. As European diseases decimated much of the Indian population, indigenous agricultural fields lay abandoned. A settler in Virginia noted the "immense quantity of Indian fields cleared ready to hand by natives, which, till we are grown over-populous, may be every way abundantly sufficient."[9] But despite these agricultural fields, indigenous American land management did not lead to the same deforestation the Europeans were accustomed to. Pioneers could drive their wagons through the spaces between the large trees. They marveled at these forests, cultivated for so long by Native Americans by intentional burning. It was said that the magnificent chestnuts were so numerous that a squirrel could travel from the Mississippi River to the Atlantic Ocean on the boughs of these productive trees. But settlers soon cleared old-growth forests of the East and Midwest for annual agriculture. It took about a century for these vast forests east of the Rocky Mountains to be replaced with acres of settlement and farmland. In the early nineteenth century Adam Hodgson wrote, "Every acre, reclaimed from the wilderness, is a conquest of civilized man over uncivilized nature."[10] This moral understanding of deforestation shows the impoverished imagination of Western civilization in its relationship to nature.

Deforestation is not the entire story, however. Cultures across the globe found ways to manage forests to be productive without completely clearing them for agricultural fields or timber use. Coppicing was one practice of managing tree varieties that resprout after being cut. These sprouted stumps, managed properly, could continuously yield timber or fiber products for hundreds of years. Across Europe, there are still stands of ancient coppiced forests. In Japan, a similar practice was followed with cedars to yield straight poles.

In the Americas, fire was the predominant tool to manage forests, but in the milpa system of forest gardening practiced by the Maya, an area of forest was cleared by hand with axes, then was burned to increase the soil fertility.[11] This area would be gardened with vegetables and planted with fruit trees, which eventually grew up and shaded out the understory. This milpa-style agroforestry yielded a diversity of products and increased the biodiversity of the landscape without leading to massive deforestation.

So the devil may not be in the ax, as it were, but rather in the ambitions of the ax wielder. This was certainly true for Gilgamesh and also seems to have been true of the colonizers of North America.

Industrial civilization only further improved the mechanical efficiency of tools. Combustion engines, fueled by cheap oil, powered chainsaws. Logging machines exponentially increased the amount of forest-clearing capacity. The last fifty years have seen as much timber logged as occurred during the entire previous history of human habitation on the earth. R. P.

Harrison reflects on this: "We call it the loss of nature, or the loss of wildlife habitat, or the loss of biodiversity, but underlying the ecological concern is perhaps a much deeper appreciation about the disappearance of boundaries, without which the human abode loses its grounding . . . Without such outside domains there is no inside in which to dwell."[12]

In 2011 I visited a Bedouin village in the Negev that, like so many other villages in neighboring Palestine, was being chronically and systematically harassed by the state of Israel. A father showed me his grandfather's deed to the land, a deed not recognized by the current regime. A grandmother pulled out a laptop and showed me video footage of her house being plowed by a bulldozer. In the evening, as the sun began to set, a young boy took me to the site of their old olive orchard, planted after the property was purchased in the 1920s. This orchard had similarly been bulldozed, an act of violence against the trees as well as an economic assault against the family. As I surveyed the scraped land, the boy walked a ways and waved me closer, beckoning me to bend my head down and look. Green shoots at our feet signaled the resprouting of some of the olive trees. My eyes adjusted to this small speck of green erupting from the reddish-brown soil, and soon my gaze caught similar shoots across the orchard. For this Bedouin boy, the sprouting roots symbolized a fragile hope in the midst of such an oppressive government.

Life persists. Notwithstanding the fateful deal with the devil that continues to plague humans with forged ax and metaled machines. Despite the decapitated head of Huwawa and severed trunks of cedars.

In the Palestinian hills, that unassuming landscape between the pyramids of Giza and the great halls of Babylon where the oldest existing tablet of Gilgamesh was pressed into clay, storytellers kept wrestling with the ongoing occurrence of the devil, that antagonizing, splinter-in-the-finger, boil-on-the-buttocks personification of lingering misery. He is the one who on the wedding night asks the bride if her love is misplaced. During the joy following the birth of a child, this adversary reminds the father that the child will experience hardship and then will absolutely die. He is not the bringer of pestilence but the consciousness of it. He does not author disease but highlights the lack of healing.

These word wranglers told another devil story, about a man named Job. In this story, the deal is not made with the man but with God. The wager this time is not about technology or a person's soul; instead it involves the soul of the world. Can this man Job continue to believe in the goodness of God when his life falls to pieces? Will he continue whistling into the dark? Or does his belief in the good depend on a fire in the hearth, mutton on the plate, and the lilting laughter of healthy children?

Whatever the answer, the devil wants to find out, so he assaults this man Job with plague, sickness, and loss of family. First, the devil takes the man's wealth through a series of thefts and disasters. Next, a storm blows over Job's house and kills his children. Finally, the integrity of his own body is attacked. Red sores bulge from under his skin; some erupt, weeping foul fluid. Job sits in ashes, in despair.

And the devil waits. Will this man metabolize grief into praise? Will he dig under the pain to find small gems of hope?

Job picks up a shard of pottery and scrapes an open boil. He looks down at his purulent legs. He looks at the pile of his former house, where death visited his children. He picks up a handful of ashes and rubs them between his fingers; some flecks fall to the ground while others burnish gray his rough skin. He responds with a small hope—not for humans, whose withering carcass of life is full of hardship from birth to death, but for trees: "At least there is hope for a tree: if it is cut down, it will sprout again, and its new shoots will not fail. Its roots may grow old in the ground, and its stump may die in the soil, yet at the scent of water it will bud and put forth shoots like a plant."[13]

Hope is a strange word, batted about in large, abstract conversations about the fate of humanity or the world. It is the question called forth by climate change, as if this one word can overcome three centuries of industrial civilization. As such, it is often used as a sort of *deus ex machina*, the magical rescue for a hemmed in storyline, a backdoor escape route for the entrapped village, a safety valve for despair.

But what if hope cannot be had? What if it resides under rocks and scuttles away when the stone is lifted? What if it keeps crawling out of the jar it was so gingerly placed in? What if its snapped-off, dried-out stem lives in a museum, while a tin statue resides in the place where hope once thrived?

Perhaps even hope for a tree is too much to ask.

As more and more trees of the American West burn every year, I wonder, will there be a last tree? Where will it live, this tree at the end of the world? Will human hands, ever hopeful for one last shade, plant it? Or will it be seeded by the last gasp of its parent plant, summoning final sap to nourish the endosperm? Will this last tree be snapped by a machine, or chopped with an ax for a final wooded fire by some desperate soul? More likely, rough winds will assail that last tree, and the beating sun will desiccate its dwindling leaves. Perhaps it too will find its resting place in a museum.

But even deeper than the root-reach of that lonely acacia, the Tree of Ténéré, life persists. Under the water table roots reach toward, below the upper layers of the earth's crust, in the caves alongside that smithy god known as Vulcan, Hephaestus, Sethlan, Ogun, and Luchtaine, lives a small hope. Down some three kilometers and more resides a thriving community of bacteria. These are not the same kind of bacteria that cause diseases, with their endless orgies of replication and division, of fast-and-loose lives multiplying and consuming as much resource as is available. No, these microbes live in the deep down, in the slow time, where life is marked in centuries. Because of sparse resources, some of these unicellular organisms undergo cell division every ten thousand years. But the secret to their tenuous existence animates the magic of their small hope: they eat minerals. They feast on metal. Armed with enzymes, these lithotrophs—literally, "rock-eaters"— sup on inorganic compounds like iron, sulfur, ammonia, and phosphorus.

And here, if anywhere, lies a microscopic hope. That in the wake of devastation caused by forged metal—the ax, the sword, the automobile, the gun—with its millennia of stumps, slaughtered sons, snapped trunks, killed children, and beheaded gods, these tiny creatures snack at the table of the blacksmith's anvil. They dull the blade with their teeth. They eat the edge of the ax.

Hope for a tree seems too heroic. Whether the lonely acacia, surviving against all odds—or the resilient olive, sprouting back to life—both seem to reflect our own desires for an
enduring promise, a beautiful persistence of life as we know
it. In light of the devastation that has come about so fully
due to our technological age, the fragility of trees, plants, and
animals in the face of the various threats haunting our world
is more realistic. We might not all make it. But those elusive
communities of lithotrophs remain, tucked away in the crev-
ices deep in the earth, shielded from the hubbub above, and
continue munching away on metal and rock, content as they
wait another ten thousand years for the advent of another cell
division, one more comrade in their struggle for life.

WISDOM DWELLS IN
DARK PLACES

The way is dark. The passage filled with edges and corners, twists and turns. We fumble our way ahead, hands muddied on the walls. Eyes are useless here. There is nothing to guide us but intuition and desire and the slap of hands against damp wall. Hungering bellies. Thirsting tongues. We breathe muggy air, hear humid whispered words: "This way." "Here." I don't know where we are, why we are here. But this one thing I know—we are groping our way forward. We are feeling our way to freedom. We are feeling. We are feeling, and because we are feeling, we will be free.

I sit up. There is no roof, only sky. My hands stretch out against nothing. I was dreaming. A billion stars overhead illuminate the rocks around me. I am not in a cave, I am in Death Valley. It is winter, and the air is cold—no clouds hang in the sky to blanket the atmosphere and keep in the warmth of the earth. I want to go back to the humidity of the cave, but instead squirm deeper into my sleeping bag.

It is the fourth night of fasting in the desert. The final night. I am here at a facilitated fast, bookended by days of sitting in circle, sharing my own story, and hearing from other participants. We gathered from across the country, and everyone came for a different reason. When asked why I am here, I struggled to articulate an answer. My reason was preverbal. In fact, it was not a reason or logic at all, it was a feeling.

After a few days of group process, we had a morning ceremony and left for our place of fasting. Mine was midway up a black crumbling mountain. I found a spot with a large dark boulder. For four days I would fast at this place, looking across Death Valley from my vantage. I would sleep under the stars and offer prayers at this big black rock, which became my anchor and altar. Here I would reflect on my life in the company of cacti and two circling ravens. On this crumbling mountain, at the base of this boulder, I would think about life and death and meaning.

Hunger leaves after day two. I still drink water when I feel thirsty, but no longer just to fill my empty stomach. My body feels a bit weaker. When I walk, my feet move more slowly, as I unconsciously conserve energy with steady and methodical steps.

I sit up again, reach for my notebook and pen lying on a flat rock next to my head, and jot down some lines:

Solitude slows the heart
Like the climb of wine
Up the spine
Black rock casts
jagged shadow under stars

With frigid toes
But head ablaze
I dreamt without sleeping
I saw visions with closed eyes
Praise the cold desert night
Praise the darkness and the light.

I think back to the circle from a few days ago, when I could not find words for why I was here. I know the answer now. I want to tell them: "I am here to excavate. To dig inside my chest and make for myself a space where I can have comfort and strength—even in solitude, even in the absence of food, even without shelter. I am here to search my own utter depth."

Lying back, I look up at the Milky Way spilling across the sky. I close my eyes and return, once again, to the cave.

I first heard about Blowing Cave in 2006. I worked for a hospital at the time, and my role was to drive patients home. Often the barrier to going home for poor and working-class patients was simply a ride, so my job was to provide that passage. Patients came to the hospital from around the state, so I drove to many remote and obscure parts of Arkansas.

One day as I took a patient past the town of Batesville, she said cryptically, "You know, there are subterranean fires underneath this town." Curious, I prodded her for more. The only explanation she would give was that near the town was the entrance to Blowing Cave, reputed to be one of the world's seven entrances to hell. I was intrigued by this local lore, of course, and when I got home I searched for more details.

Even a cursory search of Blowing Cave yields outlandish results. Stories range from Native American ghosts seen in the cave, to underground cities. One account describes encounters with a blind, blue-green humanoid subterranean species called, appropriately, "terros." These terros seem to have magical healing powers, as testified by one spelunker whose fractured leg was healed by a terro touch.

But curious as I was, I did not explore the cave myself until a few years later, when I was in graduate school. My friend Randall had explored the cave earlier, and I was itching to go with him. I did not know Randall as well back then. He is around six feet tall, with large kind eyes and a playful spirit. This was after he grew his hair out to near shoulder length but before he had dreadlocks sprouting from his head. What I knew of Randall: he climbed a lot, liked to smoke self-rolled cigarettes, and was always ready for an adventure. So naturally, when I heard he had crept about underneath the earth at Blowing Cave, I asked him to take me.

The cave is about an hour from our university, and the sun is low in the sky by the time we pull off the road and park our vehicle. A short hike through the oak woodland leads us to the gaping mouth of the cave, so large one could easily drive a car into it. From the mouth—a giant's mouth, open and hungry—the ground slopes downward toward the back. The roof of the entrance arches back and toward the ground at an oblique curve. At first glance, the cave seems merely to be a large chamber open to the world. But on walking to the craggy, dimly lit rock-face in the back I can see a passage large enough for a person to crawl through.

Here we stop for final checks. Headlamps, backpacks, food, water, roll of string, extra batteries, lighter. Briefly I wonder what it would mean to get lost, what these meager supplies would do to prolong my life. I push the thought out of my head. I look up at this doorway in the rock and feel my heart thud. This was not only my first significant spelunking adventure but also a trip a few years in the making.

An awkward scramble up the rocks and we both squat on the boulder just below the entrance. I feel a slight breeze coming from the tunnel. Randall pulls out a lighter and flicks it with his thumb. A spark and flame ensue, and the tongue flickers in the moving air. Randall grins. "Blowing Cave." He pulls out a pouch of tobacco and deftly rolls a cigarette, pulls it to his mouth, and lights it. I realize that we are not going into the cave yet.

I find a more comfortable sitting position on the rock and click off my headlamp for a moment. There is still dim light here in the back of the cave. I watch the furnace of ember at the end of the cigarette blaze with each inhalation. I note the drift of smoke away from the mouth of the tunnel. Blowing Cave, where the earth exhales.

Randall flicks the end of his cigarette. "You ready?"

"Yeah."

Randall goes in first. After his feet leave my sight, I follow. Hands first, finding purchase on the rock, then head inward, and with a twist of the abdomen I am inside. I quickly realize I need to turn on my headlamp as I enter into darkness.

This is not the clean tunnel with smooth even sides I had imagined. I am crouching to fit into the passage. The width easily accommodates me, but the stony sides feel pressing.

I want to push against the walls, to widen the tunnel, as when I could flex the cardboard of boxes brought together when I played as a child, or move the stems of brush I crawled through. But I can't. I must accept the walls and bear the psychological force of their hardness. Still, my mind presses hard against the sides, countering the unbearable pressure of this force on my psyche.

The cavern air is humid, and warmer than I expected. The passage is uneven, lumpy with rocks, and muddy. After five minutes of crouching and crawling, mud coats my clothes, backpack, and exposed areas of my skin. I follow the light of my friend ahead, occasionally seeing his shoes in front of me but more often hearing him snaking and twisting his body. Constant movement of my limbs and core has me panting for breath, and my ribs are already sore from bumping against rocks.

I will my body to become a worm. I want to dissolve my skeleton, so that my skin-bag of organs can better accommodate the lumpy texture of the passage. Instead the mineral of my bones and the mineral of the cave constantly collide, bruising the soft flesh and viscera between them. I breathe in, sinking into the moment. Exhale. Relax. Slow down. Worm forward.

We move like this for about thirty minutes, though it seems to be hours. Finally, my friend yells back that the small passage we are in has widened. I see him turn a corner and disappear. I grab an edge at the opening and pull my body through. I pull my hips under my body for a moment, glad to have the space to sit vertically and have my face more than a few inches above the muddy floor. My psyche eases, expanding into the welcome space.

Finally, I click my headlamp to brighter and look around the chamber. I am sitting on a rocky outcrop at the neck of the passage, where it widens to a large room. Just beyond my feet the rock drops about six feet to the floor of the room, filled with a pool of water. About twenty feet from me is the chamber's posterior wall, and at the meeting of the wall and ceiling is a small crevice from which a small waterfall streams into the chamber. I can't see where the water is going, but there must be an outlet, because the pool does not seem deeper than one or two feet.

Randall clicks off his headlamp, and I follow suit. I think of Wendell Berry's lines "To know dark, go dark, go without sight / and find that the night too blooms and sings / and is traveled by dark feet and dark wings." Here we sit, going dark.

Falling water pummels the pool rhythmically. Life feels simpler here. There is only the dark room, the clear pool, the water falling, and the enduring rock around us. I'd like to stay, to embrace the sound and the darkness. Here there is only sound and feeling. Is this what it feels like to be in the womb?

I remember seeing a documentary about caves filled with strange creatures. Glowworms. Blind salamanders. Blind fish. The options in this environment, it seems, are to either forgo light completely or find a way to make it yourself. I wonder if there are blind or eyeless creatures in the pool. I think of the lore about this cave. The humanoid blind terros. The gate to Hades. Now these things don't seem so outlandish after all.

As the water pours into the pool below, I think of the river Styx, with its boatman, Charon, who ferries the newly deceased across to Hades for a fee. Virgil said that he had eyes like hollow furnaces on fire. Charon, the child of Erebus and Nyx, Darkness and Night.

After a while, Randall rises to move onward through the cave. I have not noticed until he moves that the ledge we sit on slopes downward to the left and leads to a doorway opening to another chamber. I have no need for Charon here, and no coinage anyway. I get to my feet and follow, careful not to slip.

I often return to that cave in my mind. It is dark and ancient and deep. I remember the chamber with the pool and the flowing water. I hear the mesmerizing sound of the waterfall, see the clear pool below. I feel the firmness of the rock, the deep of the darkness. It is a liminal place, the threshold between the world underneath and the world above.

Plato told us that the cave is a place of constraint, where we experience only the shadow of truth. In his allegory of the cave, which is his theory of knowledge, he tells us that we are all captive within a cave. Behind us is a fire, and in front of that fire are statues. The light from the fire casts shadows from the statues onto the cave wall in front of us. What we think of as the world around us are merely shadows of the real.

Knowledge, Plato says, is turning from looking at the shadows cast on the wall to see the figures casting the shadows. To find the truth, in this allegory, would be to escape the cave altogether to enter the domain of light.

In her essay "Poetry Is Not a Luxury," Audre Lorde argues against this theory of knowledge and truth, and highlights feeling as central to understanding. She says it this way:

These places of possibility within ourselves are dark because
they are ancient and hidden; they have survived and grown
strong through darkness. Within these deep places, each one
of us holds an incredible reserve of creativity and power, of
unexamined and unrecorded emotion and feeling . . . When
we view living, in the european mode, only as a problem to
be solved, we then rely solely upon our ideas to make us free,
for these were what the white fathers told us were precious.
But as we become more in touch with our own ancient, black,
non-european view of living as a situation to be experienced
and interacted with, we learn more and more to cherish our
feelings, and to respect those hidden sources of our power
from where true knowledge and therefore lasting action
comes . . . The white fathers told us, I think therefore I am; and
the black mothers in each of us—the poet—whispers in our
dreams, I feel therefore I can be free.[1]

What I experienced in the cave was the opposite of Plato's
allegory. For me, this was a place not blinding me from truth
but, rather, allowing me to feel the truth. Darkness. The firmness of rock against my body. The pulsing of my heart, the
churning of the waterfall. These were true.

In a recent book, Robert Macfarlane explores with beautiful prose the world underneath our feet, which he calls the
underland. He notes that across time and cultures, humans
have used the underland for shelter, yield, and disposal. We
shelter what is valued: messages, art, lives, the dead. We mine
the underland for information, precious minerals or metals, or
visions. And in the underland we dispose of our wastes, our
traumas, and our secrets. He writes that here "we have long

placed that which we fear and wish to lose, and that which we love and wish to save."[2] Is it not true as well that our own bodies contain underlands, where, grown or buried, we harbor fears and traumas, hopes and desires?

So the cave liberates by providing a path inward. Where Plato saw only shadow and imitation of truth, Audre Lorde envisions a place of deep and ancient knowledge. Plato wants to free us from our embodied existence, whereas Lorde asks us to feel our bodies more deeply as a source of knowledge.

A lizard lies on a rock, taking in the heat of the sun. Suddenly a shadow blocks the sun and a hawk zips down from the sky. The reptile's reflexes kick in—nerves fire impulses to the fast-twitch muscles in arms and legs—and it scrambles down the rock throwing extremities forward and back, kicking up dust as it narrowly escapes the hawk's claws. The bird turns its wings upward and flies off, its characteristic call piercing the air.

In the 1800s a French physiologist, Claude Bernard, hypothesized that animals all have *le milieu interieur*, an internal environment.[3] The stability of this internal environment, Bernard proposed, is the basis of a free and independent life. This physiological hypothesis was the basis for what is now called homeostasis—the idea that organisms desire stability. Animal physiology internally organizes to achieve a stable *milieu interieur*, from the regulation of blood pressure, to heart and respiratory rate, to gastric and endocrine secretions. This is the calm of the lizard on the rock.

But life for all organisms also contains dangers. The lizard lives with both rock and hawk. Across species, simple

mechanisms help animals achieve internal environmental stability despite external threat as well. The physiology of freedom, according to Bernard, evolved into what we know of as
"fight, flight, or freeze" behaviors. When confronted with a
danger, the animal mobilizes metabolic resources to fight or
flee by increasing heart and respiratory rate and increasing
muscle efficiency with endogenous hormones. Alternatively,
the creature may respond by reducing metabolism with slow-
ing heart and respiratory rates in the "freeze" mechanism. This
option, which seems to be an even older evolutionary response,
occurs in situations perceived to be truly terrifying—when the
threat is that dire, the best option may be to play dead.

According to research led by Stephen Porges, mammals
have an additional physiological mechanism to manage the
interior environment. The polyvagal nerve complex connects
many vital organs, including heart, lungs, and stomach, to the
brain. In addition, the polyvagal complex joins the facial nerve
with this visceral array. With these bodily entanglements, the
polyvagal nerve complex provides physiological scaffolding
for social connection and bonding.[4]

Tightening the upper facial muscles into a smile and relax-
ing the lower muscles of the jaw indicate a calm inner state to
others. A grimace, by contrast, communicates inner discord.
Similarly, sounds made possible by innervation of the laryn-
geal and oropharyngeal musculature allows for social connection through vocal intonation. Linking face, head, voice, heart,
and gut to emotion is thus no metaphor. We feel with our
hearts and our stomach, and display emotions on our face and
our voices, because the polyvagal nerve complex makes this
possible.

We feel with our bodies. Deep breaths slow the heart and ease anxiety. Fear quickens the heart. Grief writes its poetry in the lines of the face. The *milieu interieur* is the feeling one has moment by moment, which is the sum of physiological processes in conversation with the external environment. At times the internal environment must roil with chemicals and impulses in order to quickly respond to the outer world. But always our viscera yearn for stability and calm. Mutual connection and solidarity help us overcome the everyday traumas of living embodied in this world of threats and contingencies.

There is another sense in which caves offer a space of freedom. Enslaved people in the antebellum South often dug caves to escape their oppression on the plantation. As so many creatures have found throughout time, going underneath the membrane of the ground offers protection from the dangers of life above the soil horizon.

Many enslaved people who fled plantation life remained close. Living in the woods or swamps nearby gave them freedom from the demands of masters but access to relationships and goods on the plantation. Digging dwellings in the ground enabled them to stay close to social networks while remaining invisible to masters and other white southerners who might jeopardize a runaway's freedom. In her thoroughly researched book *Slavery's Exiles*, Sylviane Diouf describes firsthand accounts of slaves who excavated their way to freedom.

The site had to meet many conditions. The easiest method was to find an existing cave that could be expanded if need be and hidden by brush or rocks. If a cave had to be dug from scratch, the best site was near a creek or river. The excess earth had to be disposed of to avoid suspicion, and with a stream nearby the dirt could be easily thrown in the running water to be washed away. After the site was chosen, the dimensions were laid out. A quilt or large piece of cloth would be placed at the entrance so that as the dwelling was excavated, the dirt could be piled onto the quilt and then taken away to a creek. Every time the site was approached, care had to be taken in order to use a different pathway, as even just a few walks back and forth in the vegetation would start to create a noticeable trail that might lead searchers to the cave. If possible, the cave would be dug directly next to a steep stream band, so that the diggers could approach the site over the rocks and thus avoid creating a trail.

Many accounts say these caves were comfortable and roomy: Martha Showvely visited her uncle's cave and noted that it was "a nice place."[5] Another slave, Arthur Greene, visited a friend's underground dwelling and commented, "Dis den was er—I guess 'bout size of a big room, 'cause dat big family washed, ironed, cooked, slept and done ev'ythin' down dar, dat you do in yo' house."[6]

How did maroons come and go from their dens without being seen? Location was key, of course, and often they would come and go only at night to minimize risk of capture. In addition, careful attention helped. Louis, who lived in a den in the woods, explained how interspecies allyship helped him: "Can't nobody come along without de birds telling me. Dey pays no min' to a horse or a dog but when dey spies a man dey speaks."[7] Certainly he was not the only underground maroon who learned birdsong to aid his evasion of captors.

Dens excavated in the vicinity of the plantation allowed maroons to be free from the oppression of plantation life while still having access to social bonds that could keep them alive. As indicated above, many who ran away and lived underground still had relationships with family or friends who could bring them food and, just as valuable, company. In the best cases, someone who got free dug a shelter large enough to bring family along. But if they left due to bodily threat or peril—an upcoming whipping, say—their ability to escape gave comfort to others still enmeshed in plantation life. One man in Virginia talked of his brother, Bob, who created a clever concealment for the door of the cave: "Ya could stan' right over dis hole an' wouldn't kno hit."[8] There was jubilation not just in knowing that someone had gotten away but also in their sly way of hiding.

Across the world, many people have used caves as a space of preservation. Caves keep caches of artifacts safe from weather or animals and hidden from other people. But in the case of enslaved people who fled, dens safeguarded their very lives. Diouf sums up the use of caves as a space of liberation for maroons: "Caves were an expression of fierce independence, and a manifestation of technical skills and resourcefulness. They demonstrated an uncommon resolve on the maroons' part to be and remain free. By the same token they were a stark illustration of the gruesome nature of slavery, as men, women, and children were willing to live underground for years in precarious, challenging, and potentially dangerous freedom rather than go back to bondage."[9]

Maroons were not the only ones to hide in caves. During the Civil War, many southerners who did not care to fight for wealthy white plantation owners escaped the draft by going underground. Their reasons were varied: probably few were true abolitionists; rather, they simply did not benefit directly from slavery and did not care to fight for a cause that only benefited southern elites. It was, as many said, a rich man's war and a poor man's battle.

David Dodge describes these hideouts in his 1891 article "Cave-Dwellers of the Confederacy."[10] He acknowledges that southern draft dodgers and defectors learned this from enslaved people or maroons. Draft dodgers had help with digging and with resources to make the damp space more comfortable. They often had family or friends who could also pitch in.

Compared to slave accounts of dens, he describes these as bleak dwellings: "Even under the best of circumstances, in the fairest, warmest weather, and in the driest soil, a cave was a dismal abode."[11] It seems that the difference in outlook lay in the vantage point. For an enslaved person escaping the plantation master, even a dripping and dark cave was a welcome space of liberation. For the white draft dodger, on the other hand, this was a gloomy but necessary travail to avoid conscription.

I wonder about the first maroon who had the vision to escape by excavating a hiding place. Where did they get this vision? How did they find the necessary resources? How many times did they fail in digging before creating an acceptable place to live? Did they get caught? What did it feel like to spend the first night in the cave? To be free of the master's eye, the labor, the whip?

Audre Lorde wrote that "in a world of possibility for us all, our personal visions help lay the groundwork for political action."[12] For the escapee, getting free and staying alive were political actions in themselves. So again, I ask, where did this vision of cave-dwelling come from? Perhaps one day a man hard at work saw an earthworm wriggle under the soil to escape the turn of the plow. Maybe the frustration of another turnip nibbled from underneath by gopher tooth brought a flash of inspiration. Or possibly his attempts to catch a rabbit for supper were foiled as he saw dinner escape into a den.

Cave-dwelling was a threshold of sorts. An in-between place, where one who lived was not quite enslaved but also not fully free. Though this liminal experience was not circumscribed by plantation rules, it still required careful attention to evading the society of enslavers. I wonder about the ways this place of escape transformed maroons by allowing them to simply be and feel outside the arena of plantation life. With a body so informed by the everyday trauma of slavery, what was it like to just sit in the darkness, free? How might this outer quiet have stabilized the escapees' internal environment?

I don't know what it is like to experience a life so difficult that living in a hole underground feels like freedom. But I have known the peace of an underground chamber. I have deprived my body of food and company in an attempt to excavate my own dark four-chambered heart, whooshing with waterfalls of red liquid.

The novelty of mammalian nervous systems is that through voice and face, we can give others a deeper understanding of our internal environment. Deep feeling becomes a reserve of deep creativity that can be shared. Cave-dwellers, both black maroons and white draft dodgers, were usually not lone fugitives; they depended on relationships in order to survive. Friends and family helped them to get food and often assisted with digging their dens. Did Martha Shovely hear a change in her uncle's voice when she visited him in that den, in that liberating darkness?

The very spread of this tool for survival became a political action: underground maroonage allowed many enslaved people to escape and became so well-known that this art of not being controlled was used by southern whites. Many personal visions—of escaping plantations, avoiding battles, or simply staying put—led to significant political outcomes. Southern whites' mass defection and dodging stunted the Confederacy's power. They did not all have to evade by going underground, but certainly the tactic was well-known in many places. By the end of the war, only 160,000 of the 359,000 on the official enlistment rolls were present. One historian, David Williams, wrote that these southern whites in opposition to the war "all but eliminated Confederate control" of the backwoods, swamps, and mountainous terrain in the Deep South.[13]

How can we pay attention to our bodies' yearning for stability, for freedom? How can we move toward that together? I return again to Audre Lorde's words of wisdom for tapping into mutually held stakes. The poor white southerner and the enslaved black southerner bore this society in different ways. This is why one would see a den as dismal while the other found in the dwelling a liberation.

Our bodies tell the truth. If people can have visions in these deep places, if they can see in the dark rather than believe the false promises of the light foisted by the white fathers, they might be able to find a common ground of mutual aid and political action. Here I again invoke James C. Scott's idea of rough terrain, his term for geographic areas that, by nature of their topography or ecology, make it difficult for empires to control the people residing there. Dens carved out by enslaved people who got away were a rough terrain of sorts. Fasting, solitude, and other practices create a rough terrain of the soul, a den where perhaps the plantation cannot reach.

The possibility of liberation from structures that suffocate is as fragile as that occasional rapture of deep feeling. One formerly enslaved person, when asked why he would risk hunger, cold, and other travails of life in the wild, responded: "I taste how it is to be free, en I didn' come back."[14]

My eyes crack open again. Overhead, stars still shine by the billions. But to the east there is a dim light behind the mountains. Dawn means the end of this foray into self-excavation. I'm not hungry, but soon it will be time to get out of the warmth of my bag. I'll pack the few things I brought—bag, pillow, notebook, pen, water—then bless the big black rock that cast shadows over me during these four days and nights. I'll walk slowly, carefully, back to base camp, where I will join the others and eat a simple meal. We will nourish our bodies and tell stories about our time of fasting in this place. There was no grand visitation by otherworldly beings—no angels, no demons. I am no shaman. I haven't been torn asunder by monsters and then knit back together bone by bone. I can't travel to other dimensions and recover souls. But I do know more intimately the dimensions of my body. I have paced out the length and width of my internal environs. I have discovered something dark and ancient and deep.

This desert time is a liminal space. The hard work lies ahead, in return to the hustle of regular life in a world that wants everything but calm and stability. As Audre Lorde said, "Our personal visions lay the groundwork for political action." Finding my own den of escape, of calm, allows me to better partner with others in moving the world toward more freedom.

I close my eyes one more time, for just a few more hours in the darkness.

We are feeling our way forward. Because we are feeling, we can be free.

REFUGE

I slip off my shoes and feel cool softness as I step onto sand. The sun has not yet risen, and the foggy marine air makes the light gray. I pick out a path among the rocks and make my way to the edge of the water. I am at the mouth of the Ventura River, where, when water is plentiful, it spills off the land into the Pacific Ocean. But now it is autumn, and it has been another drought year. Here, where the river meets the ocean, water has pooled just shy of the beach, creating an estuary.

I step into the water and feel the cold wetness lap at my ankles. I pause, my mind tracing the southward journey of this water from the headwaters in the Los Padres mountain range to the Pacific Ocean.

In the heat of summer, I hiked a section upriver with my friend Chris as we tried to reach the upland headwaters. The longest tributary of the river is called the Matillija fork. It has multiple branches, but the main one stretches approximately four miles into the mountains. A hiking trail follows this artery. Along this path the mountains are steep and crumbling. Geologists tell us that these mountains arose from the sea millions of years ago during the uplift of tectonic plates. Marine sediments created a lasagna of rock patterns. Here and there the lines bend from horizontal to vertical, sometimes even folding from ancient forces heaving and turning layers. Everywhere rocks and dirt break off the friable hillsides as the sparse vegetation struggles to keep the mountain intact. Hard rains will flood the narrow streams and wash the crumbled rocks and sediments down, eventually to the ocean. These mountains came from the ocean, and they are slowly going back.

We hike through open, scrubby brush until the trail takes us into the valleys that get progressively narrower within the steep hillsides. In places the smell of sulfur is strong. I see no tar seeps, but I remember the mineral richness of the area. Just a few miles downstream are multiple hot springs bursting from the rocks at the edge of the river. As we hike, we see places where the river seems to stop in pools. At times the water is under the surface, and later, where the bedrock allows, it springs up again.

We finally enter a valley eroded steeply from the hills. Here the dry heat of the chaparral contrasts with the cool shade along the stream. Willows, cottonwoods, and alders grow in places along its banks, giving welcome shade. Unshaded areas are thick with a shrub called mule fat. The landscape becomes alive. All around us is birdsong. Looking up, I see the cursive flight of swallows. Vibrant blue and orange dragonflies skim the surface of the water. The flat trail takes us up above the stream and back down. We begin to hop from one large boulder to another, until finally we stop at a small waterfall, Matillija Falls.

Here we take a break under an alder, happy for the shade and the cooling effect of the stream. We are, like so many creatures, using the stream as a thermal refuge in the heat of summer. Undoubtedly as the climate continues to change and get hotter, this will become more and more important. Streams and rivers like this offer a vital passage from the less-developed and cooler habitats of mountain ranges to the valleys below.

After a snack, we stand and eye the trail. To the right, a steep sandstone slab angles up above the falls. Thankfully, someone in the past tied a rope near the top to help with navigating the steep and sandy passage. One at a time, we walk up the slope supported, hand over hand, by the rope. This is the first of two rope-guided passages, and the second is even steeper. Up again, and a treacherous unsupported scramble brings us to the top of a large slab. I peer over the top and see that we are on an overhang—there is nothing on the other side to climb down. With no ropes, we cannot go farther. We move down the slab and go above Matillija Falls to a larger pool of water with a second waterfall. This is as far as we will go, trapped in a steep-sided valley. With our plan to reach the headwaters curtailed by the topography, Chris spends a moment taking a dip in the cool waters. I follow suit, dunking my body under the cool, refreshing waters.

On an autumn day, I park my car under a highway overpass up the valley from my house. Here the mountains of the river valley close in and almost meet, creating a narrow passage for the Ventura River and the highway. I walk past the bike trail and into a city park. This is where the river passes through the last mountain shoulders and opens into a wide floodplain. Today I hike alone and walk due south, with mountains flanking the river valley to the east and west. The river deepens in some areas and widens in others, fed by more mountain runoff.

This juncture where I start my hike houses an important site: the two wells from which the city of Ventura draws water from the river. These wells were recently shut down due to historically low water levels. Endangered steelhead trout, as well as a variety of other species, rely on the river to survive. Steelhead are an indicator species—their ability or inability to abide in the waters signals the overall health of the river and the watershed. Likewise, the presence or absence of water marks whether humans can survive here or so many other places in the arid West, especially as climate change stresses water dynamics that were already too complicated. Municipalities are not the only entities that take water from the river. Farms and ranches upstream draw water from it, as well as from the groundwater that feeds it. Our dwindling water supply makes clear that we must reimagine our relationship with water.

A proper river, after all, is a gerund, a verb become a noun. *Flowing* makes the water a river. The next few years, as the people of Ventura navigate how and when to draw water from the river or the surrounding landscape, will likely determine our ability to inhabit this watershed in the future.

I continue to walk downstream, and the water continues to flow, slowly. The riverbank is more dense here, and I often have to pick my passage across small rocks and boulders. Willows and alders line the water's edge. A few cottonwoods stand with bright yellow leaves. In places, thick stands of arundo outcompete all other plant species. Arundo is a problem: without natural local controls on its growth, the plant threatens to push out other riparian species and drink all the precious water. Yet it is easy to see animal trails creating hollows under the thick overgrowth.

As I hike, I occasionally see human trails through the brush leading to the water, and a few encampments are visible not far from the banks. I'm reminded that the river is a refuge not just for animals but also for displaced people. The invasive arundo seems to offer sanctuary to people experiencing homelessness, shielding their camps from the bike trail and roads. Here in the undeveloped zone of the river bottom, folks can find places to live away from the bustle and noise of the city and remain undisturbed by law enforcement. As Jennifer Mokos argues, the river bottom provides a therapeutic landscape for stigmatized people.[1]

Along the riverbank I see arroyo willows bent over from flooding. In other places short stalks appear to have taken root. Like the people who make a home along this river, the willow is a particularly resilient species. Its flexible limbs can bend in the deluge. Its marked ability to grow roots allows broken-off branches to reroot when lodged on a bank downstream.

After a few miles, I find a break in the riparian vegetation and climb up the short bank. My ankles need a break from the erratic terrain.

With my feet still in the water, acclimating to the cold, I look across the estuary and see a feathered circus of birds. Whimbrels stand at the water's edge and probe the muddy bottom with their curved beaks. Black-bodied coots swim, occasionally bobbing their white faces underwater. Terns sit, stout, and then erupt into flight with their angular wings. Just off the estuary waters, a troupe of plovers scurry anxiously across the beach. Through the mist, I see a long line of pelicans swooping over the ocean. All of these birds, like us humans, depend on these waters.

I think of all the teachers I've come across, stories and people and nonhuman kin who might help us learn to live rightly with the water: that yellow catfish and the noodling bachelor, arroyo willow and Boudicca. I step farther. I'm now in water up to my waist, and mud billows up between my feet. I shiver.

If we have any hope of living rightly, it will include an understanding of water as the foundation of our life. Tending to its circulation and grounding should be the basis of our social and political organization, just as it is already the foundation of our biochemical enlivenment. As my friend Randy Woodley says, water is the first medicine.

I take a breath and plunge into this murky water where land meets sea, this water so full of peril and pollution and promise. I emerge, sputtering from the cold, and as I stand, water drains off the green patch on my back.

NOTES

MOSSBACK

1. Sayers, *Desolate Place for a Defiant People*.
2. Redpath, *Roving Editor*, 291.
3. Byrd, *History of the Dividing Line*, 41.
4. Ibid., 40.
5. Oates, *War between the Union and the Confederacy*, 694.
6. US Congress, *Report of the Joint Select Committee*, 1229.
7. Kimmerer, *Gathering Moss*, 5.
8. Weber, *Matter and Desire*

LIKE A MOUNTAIN

1. Linda Quiquivix introduced me to the framework of "above" and "below." She is an amazing scholar whose work can be found at quiqui.org.
2. Horne, *Dawning of the Apocalypse*.
3. Dunbar-Ortiz, *Indigenous Peoples' History*, 3.
4. Scott, *Seeing like a State*, 14–18.
5. Eze, *Postcolonial African Philosophy*, 118.
6. Quiquivix, "Reparations toward the End of the World."
7. Oikonomakis, "Why We Still Love the Zapatistas."

THE WATERSHED AND THE GRID

1. Moholy-Nagy, *Matrix of Man*, 172.
2. Scott, *Seeing like a State*, 55.

3. Mumford, *City in History*, 192.

4. Moholy-Nagy, *Matrix of Man*, 172.

5. Mumford, *City in History*, 424.

6. Otis, *Dawes Act*, 10–11.

7. Barber, "Wounded Knee 122 Years Later."

8. Diamond, *Collapse.*

9. Ellul, *Meaning of the City*, 6.

10. Adams, *Heartland of Cities*, 138.

11. Barstad, "No Prophets?," 111.

12. Van De Mieroop, "Reading Babylon," 273.

13. Ibid.

14. Abram, *Spell of the Sensuous*, 22.

15. Tacitus, *Annals* 14.31.

16. Tacitus, *Annals* 14.35.

17. Dio Cassius, *Roman History*, 62.

18. Ransom, "Waters," 28.

AFTER APOCALYPSE

1. I am indebted to Katerina Friesen, from whom I first learned about the Potawatomi Trail of Death. As a descendant of settlers, she continues to advocate for decolonization as a scholar and activist. One of the many ways she has done so is by piloting an experience whereby settlers can journey along the Trail of Death in order to learn about it and hear about it from Potawatomi people.

2. Willard and Campbell, *Potawatomi Trail of Death*, 99.

3. Edmunds, *Potawatomis*, 160.

4. Ibid., 227.

5. Whyte, "Settler Colonialism," 127.

6. Edmunds, *Potawatomis*, 220.

7. Ibid., 267.

8. Graeber, *Fragments of an Anarchist Anthropology*, 25.

9. Vanderhooft, *Neo-Babylonian Empire*, 62.

10. Pedersen et al., "Cities and Urban Landscapes," 135.

11. Simpson, *As We Have Always Done*, 61.

12. "Parks Need Peoples."

13. Coordinadora de Organizaciones Indigenas de la Cuenca Amazonicas, "Two Agendas," 75–78.

14. Gross, "Cosmic Vision," 437.

15. Estes, *Our History Is the Future.*

16. *Apache Stronghold v. United States,* 519 F.Supp.3d 591 (2021).

17. "Donate."

18. "Calculate Your Annual Shuumi Land Tax."

19. "Reparations Tithe."

AN ANCESTOR, A CABIN, AND A LEGACY

1. Linebaugh and Rediker, *Many-Headed Hydra,* 15.

2. Ibid., 61.

3. Kimmerer, *Braiding Sweetgrass,* 214.

FINDING OUR WAY HOME

1. Merton, *Asian Journal,* 338.

2. Maturana and Varela, *Autopoiesis and Cognition.*

3. Weber, *Biology of Wonder,* 55.

4. Turner, *Extended Organism,* 5

5. This example and the following examples of animals extending their bodies come from Turner's *Extended Organism.*

6. Scott, *Against the Grain,* 42.

7. Mann, *1491,* 286.

8. Merchant, "Shades of Darkness," 382.

9. Cronon, "Trouble with Wilderness," 17.

10. Wengrow, "Violence into Order," 266.

11. Graeber, *Debt,* 65.

12. Scott, *Against the Grain,* 139.

13. Federici, *Caliban and the Witch,* 106.

14. Pierotti, *Indigenous Knowledge,* 29.

15. Ibid., 216.

16. "Modi's Escalating War."

17. Kimmerer, *Braiding Sweetgrass,* 215.

A CATECHISM OF KINSHIP

1. I want to lift up Pinar and So, the brilliant people behind Queer Nature, who write often and beautifully about tracking and kinship. I wrote the essay this one is based on in 2015 before reading their work, but since then I've often read what they write about experience and philosophy of tracking. While I believe the way I have framed the writing below represents my own thoughts and experiences, I also acknowledge that their work has undoubtedly influenced me. I highly recommend anything they write. You can find their writing at queernature.org, apocalypticecology .com, and instagram@queernature. Second, I want to offer gratitude to Jonah Evans, who has been the lead teacher and evaluator of track and sign courses I have learned so much in. Of course, any mistakes regarding animal tracks or sign in this chapter are my own.

2. Pierotti, *Indigenous Knowledge*, 12.

3. Brown, *Science and Art of Tracking*, 27.

4. Liebenberg, *Art of Tracking*.

5. See Uexküll, *Foray into the Worlds of Animals and Humans*; and Brentari, *Jakob von Uexküll*.

6. Henderson and Trulio, "Can California Ground Squirrels Reduce," 172.

7. Rowe et al., "Rattlesnake Rattles," 53–71.

8. Abram, *Becoming Animal*, 198.

9. Diouf, *Slavery's Exiles*, 102.

10. Heinrich, *Mind of the Raven*, 252.

11. Turner, *Purpose and Desire*, 160.

12. Strand, "Life Is Haptic." I highly recommend Strand's writing, which often intersects with my own writing and interests; it can be found on instagram@cosmogyny and at www.sophiestrand.com.

13. Weber, *The Biology of Wonder*, 28.

14. "Luther's Small Catechism."

HUNGERING BODIES

1. Hyde, *Trickster Makes This World*.

2. See Blackburn, *December's Child*.

3. Sheldrake, *Entangled Life*, 51.

4. Blackburn, *December's Child*, 227.

5. Haycock, *Legendary Poems*.

6. See Margulis, *Symbiosis in Cell Evolution*.

7. See "Sympoiesis," in Haraway, *Staying with the Trouble*.

8. McDonald et al., "American Gut."

9. Jha et al., "Gut Microbiome Transition."

INTO THE BRINE

1. Basso, *Wisdom Sits in Places*, 59.

2. This tale is adapted from Vance Randolph's telling in *Stiff as a Poker*.

3. See, for example, Wendell Berry, "The Body and the Earth," in *Unsettling of America*.

4. Berry, *Unsettling of America*, 112.

5. Thomas, "Fisher-Story," 337–40.

6. Snyder, *Practice of the Wild*, 10.

7. Lorde, *Sister Outsider*, 57.

8. Ibid.

9. Weber, *Matter and Desire*, 5.

10. See Estes, *Our History Is the Future*, for a deep analysis of Standing Rock and Indigenous Water Protectors.

11. O'Donohue, *To Bless the Space between Us*, 77.

12. Gow and Scholfield, *Nicander*.

13. Myers, *Watershed Discipleship*, 206.

14. The relevant passage is in Mark 1:4–8.

15. Thesiger, *Marsh Arabs*, 99.

16. Scott, *Art of Not Being Governed*, 3.

THE TREE, THE AX, AND THE STRUGGLE FOR LIFE

1. See Patowary, "Lonely Tree of Tenere"; and Nuwer, "Most Isolated Tree in the World."

2. Da Silva and Tehrani, "Comparative Phylogenetic Analyses."

3. Al-Rawi and George, "Back to the Cedar Forest," 69–90.

4. M. Williams, *Deforesting the Earth*, 80.

5. Ibid., 117.

6. Ibid., 123.

7. Ibid., 127.

8. Ibid., 173.

9. Ibid., 214.

10. Ibid., 276.

11. See, for example, Ford and Nigh, *Maya Forest Garden*.

12. M. Williams, *Deforesting the Earth*, 494.

13. Job 14:7–9, New International Version.

WISDOM DWELLS IN DARK PLACES

1. Lorde, *Sister Outsider*, 36–38.

2. Macfarlane, *Underland*, 8.

3. Turner, *Purpose and Desire*, 37–38.

4. Porges, *Polyvagal Theory*.

5. Diouf, *Slavery's Exiles*, 102.

6. Ibid., 105.

7. Ibid., 102.

8. Ibid., 101.

9. Ibid., 106.

10. Dodge, "Cave-Dwellers of the Confederacy," 514–22.

11. Ibid., 516.

12. Lorde, *Sister Outsider*, 113.

13. D. Williams, *Bitterly Divided*, 5.

14. Diouf, *Slavery's Exiles*, 312.

REFUGE

1. Mokos, "Stigmatized Places."

BIBLIOGRAPHY

Abram, David. *Becoming Animal: An Earthly Cosmology*. Vintage, 2011.

———. *The Spell of the Sensuous: Perception and Language in a More-Than-Human World*. Vintage, 1997.

Adams, Robert McCormick. *Heartland of Cities: Surveys of Ancient Settlement and Land Use on the Central Floodplain of the Euphrates*. University of Chicago Press, 1981.

Al-Rawi, F. N. H., and A. R. George. "Back to the Cedar Forest: The Beginning and End of Tablet V of the Standard Babylonian Epic of Gilgameš." *Journal of Cuneiform Studies* 66, no. 1 (January 2014): 69–90.

Barber, Johnny. "Wounded Knee 122 Years Later: What Has Changed, Here and Abroad?" *Indian Country Today*, December 31, 2012.

Barstad, Hans M. "No Prophets? Recent Developments in Biblical Prophetic Research and Ancient Near Eastern Prophecy." In *The Prophets: A Sheffield Reader*, edited by Philip Davies, 106–25. Continuum, 1996.

Basso, Keith H. *Wisdom Sits in Places: Landscape and Language among the Western Apache*. University of New Mexico Press, 1996.

Berry, Wendell. *The Unsettling of America: Culture and Agriculture*. Catapult, 2015.

Blackburn, Thomas C. *December's Child: A Book of Chumash Oral Narratives.* University of California Press, 1980.

Brentari, Carlo. *Jakob von Uexküll: The Discovery of the Umwelt between Biosemiotics and Theoretical Biology.* Springer, 2015.

Brown, Tom, Jr. *The Science and Art of Tracking: Nature's Path to Spiritual Discovery.* Berkley, 1999.

Byrd, William. *History of the Dividing Line and Other Tracts.* 1866.

Coordinadora de Organizaciones Indigenas de la Cuenca Amazonicas. "Two Agendas for Amazonian Development." *Cultural Survival Quarterly* 13, no. 4 (1989): 75–78.

Cronon, William. "The Trouble with Wilderness: or, Getting Back to the Wrong Nature." *Environmental History* 1, no. 1 (January 1996): 17.

da Silva, Sara Graça, and Jamshid J. Tehrani. "Comparative Phylogenetic Analyses Uncover the Ancient Roots of Indo-European Folktales." *Royal Society Open Science* 3, no. 1 (January 2016): 150645.

Diamond, Jared. *Collapse: How Societies Choose to Fail or Succeed.* Penguin, 2011.

Dio Cassius. *Roman History 62.* Accessed November 19, 2021. www.moellerhaus.com/Diocassius/dio62.htm.

Diouf, Sylviane A. *Slavery's Exiles: The Story of the American Maroons.* NYU Press, 2016.

Dodge, David. "Cave-Dwellers of the Confederacy." *Atlantic Monthly*, October 1891, 514–22.

"Donate." Association of Ramaytush Ohlone, accessed May 14, 2022. www.ramaytush.org/donate.html.

Dunbar-Ortiz, Roxanne. *An Indigenous Peoples' History of the United States.* Beacon, 2015.

Edmunds, R. David. *The Potawatomis: Keepers of the Fire.* University of Oklahoma Press, 1978.

Ellul, Jacques. *The Meaning of the City.* Wipf and Stock, 2011.

Estes, Nick. *Our History Is the Future: Standing Rock versus the Dakota Access Pipeline, and the Long Tradition of Indigenous Resistance.* Verso, 2019.

Eze, Emmanuel Chukwudi. *Postcolonial African Philosophy: A Critical Reader.* Wiley-Blackwell, 1997.

Federici, Silvia. *Caliban and the Witch: Women, the Body, and Primitive Accumulation.* Autonomedia, 2004.

Ford, Anabel, and Ronald Nigh. *Maya Forest Garden: Eight Millennia of Sustainable Cultivation of the Tropical Woodlands.* Left Coast Press, 2015.

Gow, A. S. F., and A. S. Scholfield. *Nicander: Poems and Poetical Fragments.* Cambridge University Press, 1953.

Graeber, David. *Debt: The First 5,000 Years.* Melville House, 2011.

———. *Fragments of an Anarchist Anthropology.* Prickly Paradigm, 2004.

Gross, Lawrence. "The Cosmic Vision of Anishinabe Culture and Religion." *American Indian Quarterly* 26, no. 3 (2002): 437.

Haraway, Donna J. *Staying with the Trouble: Making Kin in the Chthulucene.* Duke University Press, 2016.

Haycock, Marged, ed. *Legendary Poems from the Book of Taliesin.* CMCS Aberystwyth, 2007.

Heinrich, Bernd. *Mind of the Raven: Investigations and Adventures with Wolf-Birds.* HarperCollins, 2009.

Henderson, Lisa A., and Lynne A. Trulio. "Can California Ground Squirrels Reduce Predation Risk to Burrowing Owls?" *Journal of Raptor Research* 53, no. 2 (2019): 172.

Horne, Gerald. *The Dawning of the Apocalypse: The Roots of Slavery, White Supremacy, Settler Colonialism, and Capitalism in the Long Sixteenth Century.* Monthly Review Press, 2020.

Hyde, Lewis. *Trickster Makes This World: Mischief, Myth and Art.* Farrar, Straus and Giroux, 2010.

Jha, Aashish R., et al. "Gut Microbiome Transition across a Lifestyle Gradient in Himalaya." Cold Spring Harbor Laboratory, January 27, 2018. http://dx.doi.org/10.1101/253450.

Kimmerer, Robin Wall. *Braiding Sweetgrass: Indigenous Wisdom, Scientific Knowledge and the Teachings of Plants.* Milkweed, 2013.

———. *Gathering Moss: A Natural and Cultural History of Mosses.* Oregon State University Press, 2003.

Liebenberg, Louis. *The Art of Tracking: The Origin of Science.* David Phillip, 1990.

Linebaugh, Peter, and Marcus Rediker. *The Many-Headed Hydra: Sailors, Slaves, Commoners, and the Hidden History of the Revolutionary Atlantic.* Beacon, 2013.

Lorde, Audre. *Sister Outsider: Essays and Speeches.* Crossing Press, 1984.

Luther, Martin. "Luther's Small Catechism." Accessed May 29, 2022. https://blc.edu/comm/gargy/gargy1/ELSCatechism.htm.

Macfarlane, Robert. *Underland: A Deep Time Journey.* W. W. Norton, 2019.

Mann, Charles C. *1491: New Revelations of the Americas before Columbus.* Vintage, 2006.

Margulis, Lynn. *Symbiosis in Cell Evolution: Microbial Communities in the Archean and Proterozoic Eons.* W. H. Freeman, 1993.

Maturana, H. R., and F. J. Varela. *Autopoiesis and Cognition: The Realization of the Living.* Springer Science and Business Media, 2012.

McDonald, Daniel, et al. "American Gut: An Open Platform for Citizen Science Microbiome Research." *mSystems* 3, no. 3 (May 15, 2018): e00031-18.

Merchant, Carolyn. "Shades of Darkness: Race and Environmental History." *Environmental History* 8, no. 3 (July 2003): 380–94.

Merton, Thomas. *The Asian Journal of Thomas Merton.* New Directions, 1975.

"Modi's Escalating War against India's Forests and Tribal People." *Survival International,* accessed November 25, 2021. www.survivalinternational.org/articles/modi_war.

Moholy-Nagy, Sibyl. *Matrix of Man: An Illustrated History of Urban Environment.* 1968.

Mokos, Jennifer T. "Stigmatized Places as Therapeutic Land-scapes." *Medicine Anthropology Theory* 4, no. 1 (2020): 123–50.

Mumford, Lewis. *The City in History: Its Origins, Its Transformations, and Its Prospects.* Houghton Mifflin Harcourt, 1961.

Myers, Ched. *Watershed Discipleship: Reinhabiting Bioregional Faith and Practice.* Wipf and Stock, 2016.

Nuwer, Rachel. "The Most Isolated Tree in the World Was Killed by a (Probably Drunk) Driver." *Smithsonian Magazine*, October 24, 2013.

Oates, William Calvin. *The War between the Union and the Confederacy, and Its Lost Opportunities, with a History of the 15th Alabama Regiment and the Forty-Eight Battles in Which It Was Engaged . . . the War between the United States and Spain.* 1905.

O'Donohue, John. *To Bless the Space between Us: A Book of Blessings.* Convergent Books, 2008.

Oikonomakis, Leonidas. "Why We Still Love the Zapatistas." *ROAR Magazine*, accessed April 17, 2022. https://roarmag.org/magazine/why-we-still-love-the-zapatistas/.

Otis, D. S. *The Dawes Act and the Allotment of Indian Land, by D. S. Otis.* Edited by Francis Paul Prucha. University of Oklahoma Press, 1973.

"Parks Need People." *Survival International*, November 13, 2014. survivalinternational.org.

Patowary, Kaushik. "The Lonely Tree of Tenere." *Blogger* (blog), April 1, 2012. www.amusingplanet.com/2012/03/lonely-tree-of-tenere.html.

Pedersen, Olof, Paul J. J. Sinclair, Irmgard Hein, and Jakob Andersson. "Cities and Urban Landscapes in the Ancient Near East and Egypt with Special Focus on the City of Babylon." In *The Urban Mind: Cultural and Environmental Dynamics*, edited by Paul J. J. Sinclair, Gullog Nordquist, Frands Herschend, and Christian Isendahl, 113–48. Uppsala University Press, 2010.

Pierotti, Raymond. *Indigenous Knowledge, Ecology, and Evolutionary Biology.* Routledge, 2010.

Porges, Stephen W. *The Polyvagal Theory: Neurophysiological Foundations of Emotions, Attachment, Communication, and Self-Regulation.* W. W. Norton, 2011.

Quiquivix, Linda. "Reparations toward the End of the World." *Funambulist*, no. 30 (June 2020), https://thefunambulist.net/magazine/reparations/reparations-toward-the-end-of-the-world-by-linda-quiquivix, accessed August 18, 2022.

Randolph, Vance. *Stiff as a Poker: And Other Ozark Folk Tales.* Barnes and Noble, 1993.

Ransom, James. "The Waters." In *Words That Come before All Else: Environmental Philosophies of the Haudenosaunee*, edited by the Haudenosaunee Environmental Task Force. Cornell University Press, 1992.

Redpath, James. *The Roving Editor: or, Talks with Slaves in the Southern States.* 1859.

Rowe, Matthew P., Richard G. Coss, and Donald H. Owings. "Rattlesnake Rattles and Burrowing Owl Hisses: A Case of Acoustic Batesian Mimicry." *Ethology* 72, no. 1 (2010): 53–71.

Sayers, Daniel O. *A Desolate Place for a Defiant People: The Archaeology of Maroons, Indigenous Americans, and Enslaved Laborers in the Great Dismal Swamp.* University Press of Florida, 2016.

Scott, James C. *Against the Grain: A Deep History of the Earliest States.* Yale University Press, 2017.

———. *The Art of Not Being Governed: An Anarchist History of Upland Southeast Asia.* Yale University Press, 2009.

———. *Seeing like a State: How Certain Schemes to Improve the Human Condition Have Failed.* Yale University Press, 2020.

Sheldrake, Merlin. *Entangled Life: How Fungi Make Our Worlds, Change Our Minds, and Shape Our Futures.* Random House, 2020.

Silva, Sara Graça da, and Jamshid J. Tehrani. "Comparative Phylogenetic Analyses Uncover the Ancient Roots of Indo-European Folktales." *Royal Society Open Science* 3, no. 1 (2016): 150645.

Silver Run Forest Farm. "Reparations Tithe—Silver Run Forest Farm." Accessed May 14, 2022. https://silverrunforestfarm.org /reparations.

Simpson, Leanne Betasamosake. *As We Have Always Done: Indigenous Freedom through Radical Resistance.* University of Minnesota Press, 2017.

Snyder, Gary. *The Practice of the Wild: Essays.* Counterpoint, 1990.

Sogorea Te' Land Trust. "Calculate Your Annual Shuumi Land Tax." May 11, 2020. https://sogoreate-landtrust.org/pay -the-shuumi-land-tax/.

Strand, Sophie. "Life Is Haptic." December 1, 2021. Instagram@ cosmogyny.

Tacitus. *Annals.* Accessed November 18, 2021. www.sacred-texts .com/cla/tac/a14030.htm.

Thesiger, Wilfred. *The Marsh Arabs.* Penguin, 2008.

Thomas, T. H. "A Fisher-Story and Other Notes from South Wales." *Folklore* 16, no. 3 (1905): 337–40.

Turner, J. Scott. *The Extended Organism: The Physiology of Animal-Built Structures.* Harvard University Press, 2009.

———. *Purpose and Desire: What Makes Something "Alive" and Why Modern Darwinism Has Failed to Explain It.* HarperCollins, 2017.

Uexküll, Jakob von. *A Foray into the Worlds of Animals and Humans: With a Theory of Meaning.* Translated by Joseph D. O'Neil. University of Minnesota Press, 2010.

US Congress, Joint Select Committee on the Condition of Affairs in the Late Insurrectionary States. *Report of the Joint Select Committee to Inquire into the Condition of Affairs in the Late Insurrectionary States; Made to the Two Houses of Congress February 19, 1872; [and Testimony Taken.]: Report of the Joint Committee, Views of the Minority and Journal of the Select Committee, April 20, 1871–Feb. 19, 1872,* 1968.

Van De Mieroop, Marc. "Reading Babylon." *American Journal of Archaeology* 107, no. 2 (2003): 257–75.

Vanderhooft, David Stephen. *The Neo-Babylonian Empire and Babylon in the Latter Prophets*. Brill, 1999.

Weber, Andreas. *The Biology of Wonder: Aliveness, Feeling, and the Metamorphosis of Science*. New Society, 2016.

———. *Matter and Desire: An Erotic Ecology*. Chelsea Green, 2017.

Wengrow, David. "Violence into Order: Materiality and Sacred Power in Ancient Iraq." In *Rethinking Materiality: The Engagement of Mind with the Material World*, 266. McDonald Institute for Archeological Research, 2004.

Whyte, Kyle. "Settler Colonialism, Ecology, and Environmental Injustice." *Environment and Society* 9, no. 1 (2018): 125–44.

Willard, Shirley, and Susan Joyce Dansenburg Campbell. *Potawatomi Trail of Death: 1838 Removal from Indiana to Kansas*. Fulton County Historical Society, 2003.

Williams, David. *Bitterly Divided: The South's Inner Civil War*. New Press, 2010.

Williams, Michael. *Deforesting the Earth: From Prehistory to Global Crisis*. University of Chicago Press, 2003.

ACKNOWLEDGMENTS

I am six years old, and riding in the back seat of my family's lurching vehicle as we descend rutted dirt roads. We have just visited a family in a village in the foothills of Mount Kenya. As is customary, we have brought a gift basket to offer our dinner hosts. In return, as tradition dictates, they filled the basket with a gift to take home. So here I sit, the rough road jolting my body back and forth, with the gift of a live chicken squawking and flapping its wings at my feet with every bump in the road.

Gifts create a sort of indebtedness. Especially when the value of a gift cannot be exactly replicated, one feels a sense of obligation to the giver. In a society where gifts are regularly given, these compounding obligations tighten social bonds. Obligations, in this sense, function in a way quite true to the Latin root *lig-*, meaning "to tie together or bind." Like ligaments, gifts hold us together.

In the spirit of acknowledging gift and indebtedness, I want to thank so many who have contributed to this book.

They have read drafts, talked and struggled through ideas with me, and offered encouragement or inspiration.

My parents taught me from a young age to love stories. Dear friends Jonathan McRay and Kyle Holton have for years been conversation partners who shape the way I understand the world and who at various times have offered critical assessment of my ideas and words. Solveig Nilsen-Goodin has been a friend and mentor in so many ways. She has offered invaluable editing on drafts of many of the essays in this book and has helped me become a better writer. Josh Nason, Tevyn East, Jay Beck, and Lizz Schallert all read the first draft of this manuscript and gave me helpful feedback. Joe Voigts has been a constant encouragement throughout the project, and his literary eye is a treasure. A writing group with Adella Barrett, Katerina Friesen, and Tim Nafziger has helped me grow as a writer. They are all wonderful writers and poets and have given me excellent advice. Linda Hogan offered feedback and encouragement on the manuscript. I'm inspired by her beautiful writing and poetry. Matthew Vestuto has taught me much about this place I now live in, the land of the Ventureño Chumash. For that and for his friendship, I'm grateful. Randy and Edith Woodley were profoundly inspirational to me as I began to understand the impacts of settler colonialism. They teach with rigor and live with grace. I lift my hands to them in gratitude. Elaine Enns offered encouragement on many bike rides, especially in early stages of this project. Her own work on confronting colonial legacies is full of insight and inspiration. This book would not exist if Ched Myers had not so many years ago encouraged me to keep writing. I'm thankful for both of their examples as scholar-activists, and thinkers with feet on the ground.

Erynn Smith has been a constant support throughout. Erynn, I could not have done this without you. My deep gratitude is only matched by my deep love.

And finally, I offer thanks to the staff of Trinity University Press and their collaborators for their work in bringing this book to fruition. Steffanie Mortis Stevens patiently answered all my questions and gave valuable content feedback. Sarah Nawrocki steered the book through production. Christi Stanforth provided excellent copyediting. I have all of them to thank for the work of pruning a scraggly manuscript into a proper book.

So here I am, with a squawking bundle of words at my feet. My basket is full, and I am bound, obliged, and grateful. May the gift keep circulating.

DAVID PRITCHETT writes about land, ecology, settler colonialism, and the recovery of story and myth. He works in emergency medicine, and he holds a diploma in mountain medicine and is certified in track and sign. He lives in Ventura, California.

J. DREW LANHAM is a birder, naturalist, hunter-conservationist, and poet. He is the author of *Sparrow Envy: Field Guide to Birds and Lesser Beasts* and *The Home Place: Memoirs of a Colored Man's Love Affair with Nature*. The recipient of a 2022 MacArthur fellowship, he is Alumni Distinguished Professor of Wildlife Ecology at Clemson University.